DEMOCRATIC ADVANCE

AND CONFLICT RESOLUTION

IN POST COLONIAL GUYANA

ACKNOWLEDGEMENTS

Thanks are due to David Hinds, the General Secretary of the PNCR, the General Secretary of the PPP/C and the NDS Secretariat for giving permission to publish the statements which appear as appendices to this volume.

JUDAMAN SEECOOMAR

DEMOCRATIC ADVANCE

AND CONFLICT RESOLUTION

IN POST COLONIAL GUYANA

PEEPAL TREE

First published in Great Britain in 2009
Peepal Tree Press Ltd
17 King's Avenue
Leeds LS6 1QS
England

ISBN13: 9781845230272

ARTS COUNCIL
ENGLAND

Peepal Tree gratefully acknowledges Arts Council support

CONTENTS.

During the always very cordial process of working with Judaman Seecoomar towards the publication of this volume, we had to acknowledge the fact that the increasing seriousness of his final illness made it, in the end, impossible to complete the manuscript entirely as he wanted. Up to a certain point he was able to respond with his customary good grace to the suggestions that I was making as his editor and publisher, but there came a time when, whilst he was able to indicate his agreement or disagreement, he could not implement any of the suggestions made.

We agreed about what still needed to be done. It was an issue mainly of providing the kind of contextual matter that would have made the study more accessible to the non-Guyanese reader, as well as to the Guyanese for whom it was primarily intended. We agreed where that material was missing. Sadly, Dr. Seecoomar's state of health made it impossible to complete this work. He had wished that the book be available before the Guyanese elections of 2006, but for the reasons outlined above, this could not happen. In one of his last letters he wrote, 'I have done the best that is possible in my circumstances. Your expertise is even more important now.' This faith was too kind, and when his death came on 26 March 2006, after a losing fight with cancer borne with great dignity, publication ground to a standstill.

However, it was evident that this was too important a book not to see the light of day, and on the basis of his family's wishes and the reiteration of the expressions of trust that verbally he had expressed in my editorial skills, I have attempted to round out the book in the way we agreed should happen. I have tried very hard not to change any elements of the book's tone or the integrity of his arguments (about which in places I had and still have some reservations). What I have added is a paragraph here and there that makes the context of his argument more concrete. The largest addition is an attempt to sketch in the historical experience of local government in Guyana in Chapter Two.

One issue we discussed was the position of the real minorities such as the Amerindians, and I know that Dr. Seecoomar intended to give more consideration to the interests of this group in the argument of this book. However, I don't know how he intended to develop this strand of his argument, so it is not an issue I have attempted to take up.

Clearly, since Dr. Seecoomar's death in 2006, events in Guyana continue both to move on *and* display the appearance of a dispiriting stasis. There are a few occasions where I have added post-2006 facts where they reinforce the core arguments of the book. I have not had the temerity to guess how Dr. Seecoomar would have responded to the current emergence of electorally significant third party politics in Guyana or the signs that one of the main parties, the PNCR (People's National Congress Reformed) appears to be going through the kind of leadership crisis that may or may not result in a party split. I think the core principles developed in this volume remain pertinent, though clearly their application may require some rethinking. It was never Dr. Seecoomar's claim that this book was other than a contribution to an ongoing dialogue.

Authors customarily, after the due thanks for contributions made (as Dr. Seecoomar does in his preface), take responsibility for whatever faults remain in a book. Clearly, the author cannot do this. Suffice to say that Judaman Seecoomar should be credited with all the virtues of this book and its editor with its faults.

I can only hope that if Judaman's spirit is looking down from somewhere, he will not think the job too badly botched. For my part, it was a privilege to have known him and to contribute in a very small way to a book which expresses his love, sometimes exasperated, for his native Guyana and its people.

Jeremy Poynting
March 2009

PREFACE

This book has ended in an unexpected manner. Indeed half way through the writing it was forced to become the work of gut response to a subject I have loved with passion and devotion. The study of, and attempt to understand Guyana, must always be a challenge to Guyanese scholarship. It is only in this way that we will avoid destroying ourselves.

During the 1940s, I grew up on a sugar estate on the East Coast of Demerara in the then British Guiana. It was here that 'Lightning' had his cake shop.

In it he sold cigarettes, sweets, and bottled soft drinks. Pride of place, however, was the glass case at the far end of the counter. It had a single shelf. On top were cakes which were freshly baked and delivered by carrier bike from the neighbouring village bakery – buns, salara, butta flap, tun ova, tennis roll and sometimes chinee cake, pine tart and cassava pone.

The bottom was filled with bread rolls, a bowl of sardines mashed up with onions and pepper and a bottle of hot pepper sauce. When the sardines ran out, pepper and bread became the acceptable substitute.

From Monday to Friday, the cane cutters, other field workers, factory workers and the office workers dropped into Lightning on their way to and from work. They bought. Mrs. Lightning and the young Lightnings sold. Very little money changed hands.

He sat in a corner: watched and made mental notes of the transactions. You see, Lightning could not read and write and sold on 'trus'.

In those days, credit was not a part of the Guyanese working class vocabulary. Relationships, including business ones, were conducted on 'trus' – trust. In fact the idea of trust symbolised something far deeper than credit. It was the expectation and confidence that neighbour would do right by neighbour in all their encounters.[1]

Saturday was payday. On their way from the pay office, workers dropped in again. This time they came to pay their bills.

"How much?"

"Eighty-seven cent."

"Nah maan, da tuh much."

Lightning then came into his own. He drew himself erect.

"Monday yuh tek four cigritte, one sardine an bread, one coke. Dah is 16 cent.

"Tuesday, half pack Lighthouse, two peppa an bread an one pepsi. Dah mek…" And so he recounted each item, for each day, to the nearest cent.

They paid.

His customers rarely questioned his accounting. The trust was mutual.

This cameo, with or without the agile memory, was replicated several times over in every village, estate, and settlement, throughout the land. It was a measure of the closeness of rural community life in action, even though it did not always mean total honesty.

From the 1960s onward, political change seemed to bring with it a growth of hustle, selfishness and nagging uncertainty. Brother began to suspect brother. Friends began to be uneasy in each other's company and neighbours began to mistrust each other. Today, it seems that the public philosophy enshrines internecine violence as the only means to conduct relationships and deal with human conflict.

This work sets out to explore the reconstruction of trust as a condition of democratic engagement and self-sustaining peace. For without this, Professor Premdas's prophecy of a doomed Guyana threatens to engulf us all in terror.[2]

Incidentally, Lightning did not get his name because of his amazing mental agility. No. It came from something much more mundane. Side by side with his shop keeping, Lightning operated a local transport facility. He had a cart and two donkeys and fetched goods for whoever would hire him. However much they were prodded, the donkeys moved at one s-l-o-w and s-t-e-a-d-y pace.

One day the local estate wit, unable to bear it any longer, blurted out;

"Man Mohan, yuh dankey ah move like lightnin." And so from that day onward Mohan became 'Lightning'.

Before independence in 1966, colonialism embodied the public philosophy in Guyana. The colonial authority made the controlling decisions and the peoples' obligation was to obey or be coerced into compliance. They were deemed too unschooled to take part. Even the moves toward democratically elected village councils, as the twentieth century progressed, was mocked by the retention of financial control at the centre.[3] Fiscal policy invariably favoured the plantation at the expense of the village.[4] Government was therefore remote – a thing apart – from which, as a measure of defence, they expected nothing. As an imposition, authority was there to be dodged, deceived, resisted, or outwitted as a legitimate means of survival.

Privately, however, the people took their cues from their Gods and the wisdom and guidance which their elders, religious and educational leaders provided. Whether the deity was African or Amerindian, Chinese or Christian, Hindu or Muslim, the common exhortation was the brotherhood of man, love, respect and care for others. Honesty and the bond of one's word provided the anchorages for personal relationships and the protective shield against the injustices of a demeaning, authoritarian political system. This was the moral value system by which the people organised their private and communal lives and rescued themselves from spiritual defeat. These were group preserving beliefs and practices. They also formed boundaries within which the stereotypes, suspicions, and fears of the 'other' took root and grew. Inevitably, with proximity, there was spill over at the individual level but these were never widespread enough to threaten the prevailing misunderstandings. Indeed, both in the break-up of the sugar estate communities in the 1950s and the establishment of the largely single ethnic extra-nuclear villages, and then in the subsequent flight of one or other of ethnic groups from the fringes of these villages during the racial disturbances of the early 1960s, residential segregation became more, rather than less marked. It is the permeation of boundaries and the development of understanding and a common will which embody some of the greatest challenges to Guyanese thought and action as they pursue a better society.

With independence, the responsibility for public decisions now fell to the people and their chosen representatives – by default – to the Guyanese political elite themselves. Alas! Behind a high sounding façade of empty socialist rhetoric, they vied with each other to don the colonial mantle in a grotesque interpretation of the good life for the few. Thirty-eight years on, Guyana might be expected to be accumulating wisdom and approaching some semblance of maturity. Yet, a Guyanese identity has not even been conceived and it appears that all passion was spent on inducing the birth of the country. The Guyanese leadership has been unable to transform the liberal democratic institutions for which they clamoured into a functioning political system. They have been incapable of articulating a coherent set of principles to guide public life, to set acceptable common goals for all, or to design institutions or devise practices which encourage active cooperation and deliver on the people's welfare.

What has emerged out of this intellectual and creative vacuum has been confusion and uncertainty. Instead of cooperative moves towards agreed goals, the country has split along ethnic lines and politics reduced to an indecent struggle for group supremacy. In the shadowy recesses of some minds is the question, *Whose space is it anyway?*[5] Should 'interlopers' be suppressed, dominated, or ethnically cleansed in some other way? In this primeval encounter, the guidance of religion has been submerged and men and women seem to have lost their reason and are floundering in ever decreasing circles in a sea of anxiety, frustration, and stupefaction.

What appears to be missing is a publicly articulated philosophical position to guide our political life and upon which the people can debate, raise dissenting voices freely, and refine continuously. Instead, what passes for political dissent in Guyana is frequently just the myopia of ethnocentrism, focusing as it does on the unfitness of the 'other' to hold power, and rarely on the appropriateness of the institutions for a divided society. It is this theoretical emptiness which makes our institutions rootless, without ideational foundations and subject to the buffetings of all comers. For in Michael Sandel's words, "Political institutions are not simply instruments that implement ideas independently; they are themselves embodiments of ideas."[6]

This study attempts to join the debate on the reconfiguration of social and political life in Guyana by raising the possibilities for democratic ideals and their institutional adaptations in a warring multi-ethnic society. It assumes that the majority of Guyanese wish to work out a system for peaceful social coexistence in their country, a system, which might eventually lead to all groups embracing the proposition that difference in purposive interaction enriches and expands human experiences and understanding.[7] How in other words do we set out to breathe new life and meaning into our grand design – The Cooperative Republic? Remembering that at birth the public philosophy of the new Republic was to make the "small man a real man" and that this awesome task of human development was to be entrusted to Cooperatives[8] and the culture of Cooperation which would come with them. Cooperatives died in infancy and the small man/woman has not yet been liberated, let alone become the much vaunted independent citizen.

In regenerating our society we have to remind ourselves that the Republic as philosophy and practice enshrines "the idea that liberty depends on sharing in self government... Sharing in self-rule means deliberating with fellow citizens about the common good and helping to shape the destiny of the political community... To share in self-rule therefore requires that citizens possess, or come to acquire certain qualities of character or civic virtues... [and this in turn] requires a formative politics, a politics which cultivates in citizens the qualities of character self-government requires."[9]

It is my belief that out of all this renewed effort might come the realisation that to be Guyanese is not to be some mythical cultural hybrid;

- that society is a complex of diverse identities, each valid in its own right and capable of cooperating for the greater good;
- that in the process of cooperation a core set of values, attitudes, and beliefs, dedicated to the greater good, might grow and the transition from subject, to citizen, to people might take place;

- that one can be African, Amerindian, Chinese, Indian, Portuguese and all the other possible combinations and also be Guyanese, and at peace with one's self.
- that out of this dynamism might emerge commitment and trust, which are the bedfellows of a functioning democracy; and
- that out of this process of coexistence might emerge a leadership which honours the differences of a plural society and measures its every action against the test of need satisfaction of all its people.

I wish to thank –

The Institute of Commonwealth Studies for granting me a two-year Visiting Fellowship. This allowed me invaluable access to the Research Libraries in London.

My daughter Fidel for rescuing the idea and making it all happen.

My other daughters Agnes and Nadira for giving encouragement and practical help throughout the writing process.

My grandchildren Mercedes, Oliver, Sebastian and Isabella for providing encouragement in their own way.

My brother James for reading the manuscript and offering valuable comments along the way.

My friend Kampta, as usual, read, commented on and provided general help with the entire project.

My friends and relatives: Peter and Savi Jailall provided immense support and encouragement for the writing and completion. In their own way Lance and Mivvi Jaundoo, Kwamla and Agnes Atteen, Marcia Inasi, Asha Jaundoo, Leila and Hackim Ali, Nick Laughland, Kate Sprecher, Dr. Kerryn Lutchmansingh, Melinda Janki and Desmond Bermingham all affected the outcome of the current study.

The responsibility for the work is entirely mine.

Judaman Seecoomar, May 2005.

END NOTES

1. For a learned exposition on the notion of Trust as social capital and its role in economic development see Fukuyama, F. (1995), *Trust: The Social Virtues and the Creation of Prosperity,* NY, Simon and Schuster Inc.

2. Premdas, R. (2001), 'Ethno-Racial Divisions and Governance', *Racism and Public Policy, (Conference Paper), p.* 38, Geneva, UNRISD.

3. Rodney, W. (1981), *A History of the Guyanese Working People, 1881-1905,* London, Johns Hopkins University Press, pp.133-135.

4. Adamson, A. H. (1972), *Sugar Without Slaves; The Political Economy of British Guiana, 1838-1904,* New Haven, Yale University Press, p.256.

5. At regular intervals, some African Guyanese use the letters columns of the local newspapers to remind the Indian Guyanese that they are living on African ancestral lands. They base this on longer residence and the amount of labour extracted from their forefathers to make the country both habitable and productive. The 1980 Guyana Constitution enshrines equal rights but such a claim needs attention lest it become a battle cry in times of trouble.

6. Sandel, M. (1996), *Democracy's Discontent,* p. ix, Camb., Mass., Belknap Press.

7. Taylor, C. (2001), 'A Tension in Modern Democracy' in Botwinick, A. and Connolly, W. E. (eds.), (2001), *Democracy And Vision: Sheldon Wolin and the Vicissitudes of the Political,* Princeton, Princeton University Press, pp. 88-95.

8. Burnham, F. (1970), *A Destiny To Mould,* New York, Africana Publishing, p. 70.

9. Sandel, M. (1996), pp 5-6.

CHAPTER ONE.

INTRODUCTION

"The burden of our findings is that there can be no economic solution without a political solution."
                    Caribbean Conference of Churches, (1991).

1 Overview

Guyana is a colonial creation. Today it is a deeply divided and floundering multi-ethnic state which is in the throes of working out a viable post-colonial identity. It was originally carved out of the Northern South American Guyana plateau by the Dutch as three river colonies – Essequibo, Demerara, and Berbice. They were ceded to Britain in 1803 as part of the settlement which followed the Napoleonic wars and were united in 1831, by British administrative action, as the colony of British Guiana. It remained a possession for plunder for 135 years until independence on May 26, 1966.

Like the land itself, the population was also a feat of colonial engineering. From the seventeenth to the first quarter of the twentieth century, hundreds of thousands of human beings were ferried across the oceans to labour, first on the Dutch and then on the British plantations. They came literally, and then legally bound, from Africa, India, Madeira, and China, among other countries, to produce that surplus which played no small part in the financing of the first British industrial revolution.[1] In excess of ninety per cent of today's population are the descendants of those immigrants. Most of the others are the continent's indigenous Amerindians.

British colonial policy supported the notion that competing races ensured the safety of the white minority and so in promoting that competition, the seeds of suspicion, resentment and fear were deliberately pursued as principles of good governance. This 'divide and rule' culture was buttressed by that other dictum which proclaimed that social order demanded that the ruling group enforced its control ruthlessly.

By the time independence came, the doctrine of competing races had hardened into a politics based on the struggle between the parties supported by African and Indian Guyanese for the control of the State, its resources and its status distributions. Included in the latter are those important and much trampled upon human existential needs of identity, dignity, self esteem, and pride.

Ignoring the lethal intensity of inter-ethnic competition, the departing coloniser collaborated with local demands for constitutional instruments and institutions which fostered zero sum adversarial politics, ethnic antagonisms and encouragements to violence as legitimate means to resolve conflicts. Independence also came at the height of the Cold War. This total drive to defeat communism consigned one Marxist party and one ethnic group to the political wilderness. It also provided the cloak for political skulduggery, the opportunity for the attempt to promote the welfare of one group at the expense of the others, and the disincentive to set goals and develop practices for the liberation and growth of a new kind of fabricated society. The lacerations in the social body widened.

The first phase of independence, dominated by one political party and one ethnic group, (The Peoples National Congress (PNC) and its mainly African support base) ended in 1992. The end of the Cold War restored electoral democracy as the primary virtue rather than support for a variety of anti-communist tyrannies. It allowed the group which had spent 28 years in opposition, the Peoples Progressive Party (PPP) and its mainly Indian constituency, its Marxism allegedly intact,[2] to take control of the government. Alas! Whatever policies the PPP brought to the issues of economic development, (their strategy was essentially to maintain the economic liberalisation begun by

Desmond Hoyte following the death of Forbes Burnham in 1985), they arrived from the political sidelines without a single new idea about how to confront the dilemmas of a fractured multi-ethnic society. And the lacerations continued to widen.

Twelve years and three elections into this second – post Cold War phase – Guyana and its government continue to flounder in the gap between its ethnic cleavages. Still mired in the ethnically driven politics of government and opposition and despite claims to multi-ethnicity,[3] the government finds itself with an electoral majority (mainly from one ethnic group) and legal responsibility but without the power, authority, or legitimacy, to govern effectively. These latter bases of power are in the gift of the opposition. It has used them ruthlessly for the sole purpose of attempting to overthrow what it declares to be a corrupt and incompetent government. What complicates matters is that the two main political parties have their power bases in different sections of the social structure, the PNC in the public services and the PPP in the economic heartland. When in opposition either party can and do wreak havoc with economic growth and political stability.

Since 1992, the political arithmetic stacked against them, the Guyanese Opposition Party, the PNCR, developed a strategy and a discourse to counter this electoral disadvantage. The navigation points of this new manifesto involved withdrawal from 'loyal' opposition in parliament to the political margins (in 2002, the PNC withdrew from parliament for eleven months), support for street violence (and an ambivalence with regard to those involved in criminal conspiracy) all with the implicit intention of making the country ungovernable – fire! – slow fire!! – mo fire!!! – and negotiations from strength. (The logic and dangers of this design for action will be examined in some detail later.) For now, however, the impact of such uncompromising opposition on the operating psyche of the environment must be noted.

In such an open season, other disturbing elements stepped into this arena of growing political anarchy. Whether by invitation, tacit support, opportunist muscling in or just a wicked desire to join in and intensify the mayhem, they have come like tropical beetles to gaslight in the dark night: heavily armed bandits, drug barons, and petty criminals, posing as champions of the marginalised, cry liberation! and kill at will. They rape, kidnap and plunder with impunity, while an irresponsible media stir up communal hatred in the name of public debate. Politics, crime, and bloodlust have become hopelessly intertwined.

What was toxic, but not new, in this mix was the racialisation of crime. Whilst no doubt much of the new criminality was intimately connected to narco-trading, there were attempts to grace some of this criminality with the badge of being a legitimate defence on the part of African Guyanese against an elected PPP/Indian dictatorship. A break-out from Georgetown Prison was labelled as 'The Five for Freedom' whose mission was to defend the rights of the Afro-Guyanese. A spree of killings targeted officers in the police force and a disproportionate number of Indo-Guyanese. Also in 2002, there was an armed attack on the Office of the Prime Minister in which two state officials died. The village of Buxton-Friendship became a no-go area for the police and the centre for attacks on mainly Indo-Guyanese villages. Threats to respond in kind from neighbouring Annandale raised the spectre of a return to the ethnic conflicts of the early 1960s. Support for these 'liberation' forces came from TV talk shows and in the view of the government, there were PNCR activists involved in the giving of, at the very least, moral support.[4] In turn, organisations such as the Guyana Indian Heritage Association issued starkly accusatory papers on the racial basis of crime in Guyana, and though other organisations such as the Guyana Human Rights Association(GHRA) and the Guyana Bar Association challenged any simple relationship between ethnicity and crime, it was what people believed that constituted an incendiary discourse.[5]

What equally concerned the GHRA was the upsurge in extra-judicial killings whose victims were predominantly young Afro-Guyanese. In 2002, at least twenty such killings were recorded, allegedly at the hands of the TSS (Target Special Service) unit. The government's minister for Home Affairs, Ronald Gajraj, was forced to resign, and although subsequently cleared of involvement, there was enough disquiet aroused for the US

Government to revoke his visa. Nevertheless, the perception was widespread amongst many Guyanese that the government had countenanced such measures because of its perceived failure to protect its core Indian supporters. Establishing the whole truth in such matters is probably impossible. What was incontestable was that amid all this death, destruction, and disillusion, the rest of the society became shocked, uncertain, afraid and frozen and the government, meanwhile, was seen as unable to perform that most fundamental obligation of protecting its citizenry, and amid the charges of racially motivated extra-judicial killings, had all but lost its moral claim to govern.[6]

It is no consolation to the Guyanese to point out that the pattern of communal conflict in their country is not unique, that it has been replicated in most of the post-colonial civil wars since the end of the second world war and has become dominant in the politics of today's post Cold-War world. These are consequences of the refusal to accept authoritarian exclusion by hitherto subject minorities, the stalled process of transition from subject, to citizen, to people within existing multi-ethnic societies, and the demands of these identifiable groups[7] for greater democratic involvement. Any study of Guyana, its racial divisions and the struggle by ethnic-based political parties to control the state and its distributions, contributes to that more general understanding of ethnic diversity, its political cleavages and democratic participation in a free society. In this sense, study of Guyana is a metaphor for other multi-ethnic post colonial states.

The pressing question for Guyana is this: Is it at all possible to stop the seemingly inexorable slide into civil war in the name of democratic advance and for ethnic groups to achieve their aims by more peaceful and constructive means? If so, how is this new democracy to be organised so that all Guyanese are recognised and allowed to share equally in decisions which affect their welfare?

In an earlier study[8] I suggested that amid all the chaos, fear, resentment, suspicion, and mistrust, hatred had not yet become all consuming. This allowed that proverbial window of opportunity for dialogue, negotiation and consensus before death and destruction begin their self-generating existence.

Following John Burton and his colleagues, the argument went like this:

- all Guyanese, like all other human beings, have certain existential needs which have to be satisfied if conflict is to be managed and social order maintained. In other words, conflict ensues if these needs are consistently denied or perceived to be denied;
- these needs include the need for Justice, Equality and Human Dignity, which are, of course, also the proper ends of a democratic society. The means to these ends have been conjectured as the satisfaction of the needs for security, recognition, participation, identity, and distributive justice. Corroboration for this proposition comes from conversations with Guyanese, the philosophy of science, theories of learning and socialisation, and modern and postmodern thinkers on society and human behaviour;
- resolution then becomes a matter of creating the conditions for need satisfaction. This means designing institutions and developing practices which set out to do just this and in the process provide opportunities for functional cooperation and the growth of a common will;
- to provide the environment for this challenge to the creative imagination, Burton and his colleagues resurrect the age-old strategy of collaborative analytical problem-solving. This is facilitated dialogue which is so organised that those in conflict are encouraged to convert the things which divide them into problems to be solved. They can then begin to make those choices which might allow them to satisfy their needs and coexist peacefully.

The theoretical scaffolding for this deceptively simple set of actions was developed in the previous study.[9] The parties to the conflict were identified. The nature of the conflict was historically located, analysed and defined. Some Guyanese were enrolled as partners in the search for understanding and resolution. Propositions for resolution were laid out, and enabling techniques were discussed both as simulations and operations in the field. In the end it was suggested that social organisation which was undergirded by a focus on need satisfaction for all, was also the foundation for the peaceful handling of social change, the growth of participative democracy, and human development in its widest sense

For a number of practical reasons not every aspect of that theoretical outline could be developed in the earlier work. This book therefore sets out to turn its attention to participative democracy, as distinct from electoral democracy, and institutional change as essential contributors towards that human development which is the avowed end of all political activity.

More than fifty years ago, the Guyanese independence movement, with great foresight, set itself a goal. It was summed up in the high sounding rallying cry "One People, One Nation, One Destiny". It was probably their only act of prescience. They had realised implicitly at least, that different peoples with different goals would produce a state in deep trouble. It is less clear whether the makers of that slogan had foreseen that without single-minded determination and relentless hard work to forge a working political will, democratic legitimacy would be its first victim.[10]

More than thirty-five years ago, the Republic of Guyana was proclaimed. Cooperation and Cooperatives were to be the road on which the Guyanese would travel toward that 'unity in diversity'. But instead of creating the conditions for the flowering of cooperation, the Guyanese turned back to their colonial experience for guidance on governance. One group after the other sought to take power and enforce it with as much steel as they could muster. All have failed.

The book sets out to argue for a revaluation of the target of cooperation. In doing so, it focuses on the human need for participation within a democratic framework which is inclusive and committed to a minimum set of redefined and redesigned common goals.

This is a monumental task. I have attempted to lay out as many paths to cooperation and from as many sources as is possible in the hope that these might then assist the people and their chosen representatives to make choices which are mutually satisfactory. There are easier and more gruesome alternatives. These include variations on the themes of civil violence, ethnic cleansing, and even conquest by Guyana's more powerful neighbours. These outcomes would only serve to create more problems, not solve them.

Without a fundamental redirection of efforts, violence would seem inescapable in Guyana. The history of the country has been tied up with it. Slavery, indenture, and colonial rule were violent in their operations and in their structure. There was pre-independence civil war and post-independence banditry to which the state turned a blind eye. In fact banditry has been a growing phenomenon of Guyanese life and from 1992 onwards, a coherent discourse of political violence has been developed as grounds for a set of extra-parliamentary actions in the name of political advance. Violence is now the undeclared rationale of open political discourse.[11]

The signposts of that discourse have already been noted.[9] Parts of this book will trace its development and examine the legitimacy of violence as a strategy for democratic inclusion. It will analyse the inherent dangers in the sponsorship of a culture of violence and suggest an alternative framework in which democratic progress might be possible without further demonstrations of man's inhumanity in the name of justice.

The challenge which Guyana faces in 2005 and beyond is: How does the country use its post-1992 freedom to control itself humanely? That is, after the subordinations of colonialism and the cold war have ended? How, in other words, do we confront our diversity and organise it so that the acts of government have legitimacy, cooperation is encouraged, and coexistence grows into something more substantial – the emergence of a common will?

This book makes the assumption that it is not beyond the wit of Guyanese to devise institutions and procedures which will set us on the road to a functioning, participative democracy. It is about road building in one country and demonstrates one set of institutions, procedures, and functions for the trans-formation of a variegated colonially-created society into a working multi-ethnic democratic Republic – one in which common aims are pursued so that all might benefit.

2. Democratic Shadows in Guyana: A Preliminary Discussion.

In the chapter which follows we will discuss the idea and meaning of democracy, and the human and institutional demands that have to be met if it is to become an acceptable system of good governance. For now, it it is useful to trace the historical trajectory of the claims to democracy throughout the country's political life.

The first 122 years is the story of unrelenting colonial rule. For the overwhelming majority (95%) of the population, it is the experience of being subjects, stamped with inferiority and without any promise of participation, liberty or equality. During the next 13 years (1953-1966), the local political leadership, spurred on by notions of freedom and self-determination, underwent an apprenticeship in participation under the grudging tutelage of the colonial ringmaster. From 1966 onwards, an independent Guyana acquired and then devised institutions based on a majoritarian interpretation of democracy. These, in a situation where majority rule threatened permanent power in the hands of one group, whether by electoral fraud or leveraging ethnic loyalties, had failure written all over them. The periodic change of government by electoral means that is a fundamental requirement of a functioning democracy did not happen. Political life became exclusive, adversarial, and destructive.

It is worth mentioning at this point that the ethnic distribution of the Guyanese population in 1953 was 35% African, 4% Amerindian, 46% East Indian, 2% European and Chinese, and 11% Mixed race.[13] The 2003 figures are 43% Africans, 4% Amerindians, 51% East Indians, 2% European and Chinese.[14] In the latter set of figures the mixed group (the group that in the old censuses was defined as 'coloured') has disappeared into the main ethnic groups, especially the Africans. The PNCR believes that it is this Indian ethnic majority and its voting loyalties which condemns it to seemingly permanent opposition.

This has indeed been the pattern of succeeding elections since 1992. In 1992, on a badly defective electoral register, the PPP/C obtained 53.5% of the vote, the PNC, 42%. Even when the electoral register added a further 77,286 electors (an increase of over 20%), by 1997, the percentage breakdown of votes cast was 55.26% to the PPP/C and 40.5% to the PNC. In 2001, the difference had changed very little: 53% to the PPP/C and 41.8% to the PNCR. (In 2000, the PNC rebranded itself as the PNC Reform.)[15]

Whilst this succession of results could not be said to support the PPP/C's claim that it had a significant appeal beyond its ethnic base, it was very clear to the PNCR that they were never likely to win an election again. Sections of the PNCR, therefore, saw extra-parliamentary opposition, and the destabilisation it produces, as the only way to counter marginalisation and non-recognition, and to negotiate change from a position of strength. As true of all parties, particularly those based largely ethnicity, the PNCR has always been a coalition of interests, and it is possible to see two wings of the party in a somewhat cynical embrace. One section of the Party began to argue in a high-minded way for power sharing based on the Lijphartian model of the 'Grand Coalition' (See Chapter 3 for a discussion of power sharing models), whilst another section of the party was prepared to support violent extra-parliamentary methods to influence the debate.

The fragility of democracy or the shallowness of its roots has a long history. The journey on the fringes of democracy began in 1953 when postwar international and British domestic economic pressures for disengagement from empire began to gather momentum. Universal adult suffrage was granted where formerly only the select few had access to the vote. Twenty-four defined constituencies were proclaimed and the people were invited to vote for their representatives. The prize was a degree of influence over domestic affairs in a hybrid colonial system in which the colonial government maintained control of the public service, external affairs, police, defence, finance, and law and order and even in domestic affairs the colonial governor had considerable "powers of suspension, veto, and certification".[16]

Contrary to expectations that the Guyanese would do what they were told and return officially-supported 'safe hands', they voted solidly (18 out of 24 seats) for the party which had spent years educating them about the evils of colonialism – the ethnically 'co-operating', self-proclaimed Marxist Peoples Progressive Party, (PPP). This was too much for a reluctant emancipator to bear and in pasture cricket terms the owner of the ball gathered it up in a fit of pique and abruptly ended the game. After 133 days the constitution was suspended and the PPP, like wayward schoolboys and girls, was ejected from power, and some of its leaders detained. The alleged reason was the claim that the PPP was planning to establish a one-party communist state – the evidence, the intemperate language of some ministers. The real reason – at the height of the cold war – was that there was no room for even a left-leaning state not reliably obedient to State Department interests in America's backyard. It was to be Guyana's one true moment with democracy. The people had voted openly. They had chosen the representatives to govern them and were told, No! Fifty years on, the legitimacy of 1953 continues to be elusive and political life degenerates daily.

And then, in a perfect demonstration of how a pseudo-democracy should be constituted and run, the colonial Governor, with London's consent, proceeded to nominate an interim government comprised largely of those who had been defeated in the recent election. In terms of their march to independence, the Guyanese were now to return to their starting positions and mark time for an indeterminate period. Governor Sir Patrick Renison captured the bathos in grand imperial style when he said, "As any soldier knows, marking time is not like standing still. On suitable ground it can make a great impression."[17]

Renison was right. Marking time did make a profound impression on the political landscape of Guyana. The PPP split into ethnically identifiable groupings, the people turned inward and the downward spiral in Guyanese political life began.

The march to independence on the "Queen's Highway"[18] was resumed in 1957. The Governor, his colonial officials and their nominated ménage now retained a much higher degree of control over the elected members. This was because the British Government could not risk a second collapse and so would not restore the suspended constitution. The constitutional instruments were different from 1953 but they did not take into account the changed nature of the political environment. This meant, therefore, that as long as race continued to be the determining factor in political behaviour, only one group, with its built-in majority, could govern. The other group, the African Guyanese faced exclusion and permanent opposition. Everything was viewed through the prism of race and in time frustration led to public protest and violence.

In 1957 the Indian-supported PPP won a majority of seats at the elections and assumed ministerial responsibility for the assigned portfolios. The African supported Peoples National Congress (PNC) was cast in the role of opposition. Ostensibly, at the beginnings of their separation, both parties claimed to be multiracial and offering different kinds of socialism. As such they could hope to be alternating governments. Soon, however, they were branded the Coolie party and the Black man party. Everything the one did was to be condemned by the other, and 'making the country ungovernable' became the objective of political opposition. To this day, this remains the case.

The 1961 constitution provided for the protection of human rights and for the additional transfer of responsibility from the Governor to the elected ministers. The 1957 pattern repeated itself. The PPP won again and the alarm bells grew louder. Independence was now in sight and the PNC was determined that the Indian-led PPP should not lead the country into freedom. It used its ethnic support from the public services, the Georgetown working class and the forces of law and order to deadly effect. There were other forces at work. The right wing United Force (UF) party (whose powerbase lay in the Portuguese middle class) wanted nothing to do with godless communism, while the United States of America was in no doubt that an independent Guyana should not fall into the hands of communists. The British gave silent support to these pressures. Together, these forces of opposition set out to fabricate a change of regime and they used inter-group violence as the means to its achievement. The first half of the 1960s was dominated by protest marches, strikes, riots, burnings, looting, and killing. Racial uncertainties and rivalries were ruthlessly exploited and in the end a changed voting system – Proportional Representation – was imposed to engineer a coalition government to replace the PPP in 1964.[19]

It bears re-emphasis that the 1957-1964 period was not an encounter with democracy, nor a serious preparation for independence. If it was anything at all it provided some departmental management experience for the few and engendered immense internecine bitterness and confusion. Opposition politics as politics of the street had taken firm root.

3. Democratic Institutions and Political Behaviour.

In 1966, after a turbulent seven year period of experimentation under two PPP governments with some self-governing institutions and two years of comparative calm under the PNC and UF coalition, Guyana was granted independence. It demanded and got a constitution modelled on Westminster style democracy, complete with instruments of government and opposition in a deeply divided society. Only the voting system was changed and the regret must be that the opportunity was missed to devise a different democratic system for an artificially created society. Guyana, as a racially polarised colonial society, became an independent state with a wholly inappropriate class-based constitution which had taken its originators hundreds of years to develop in its own setting.[20] It was as if the departing colonial overlords needed to prove that their contentions about inherent inferiority and incompetence were well founded, and that the ghost of 'divide and rule' would continue to haunt us for years to come. It is worth a mention that in 2003, somewhere in the dovecotes of the chancelleries of the West, the notion of 'failed democracies' flutters gently. It is the old and new imperial powers thinking seriously of resuming where they left off – this time in the name of making the world safe for democracy.[21] The choice is stark. Are we going to invite re-colonisation through inaction? Or can we give life to institutions which will manage our independence and guard our freedom from the tentacles of the new imperium?

During the last half century the notion that traditional democratic institutions produce democratic political behaviour has been cruelly exposed. We have witnessed for too long the activities of government designed for its own benefit and the benefit of its chosen few. What was on show was the primacy of power. It was certainly not democracy. This divorce of people from a succession of governments has generated fraud, sabotage and the joy of outwitting authority as legitimate forms of counter behaviour. It should not be surprising, therefore, that governments seen as rooted in one ethnic group have received the same treatment from those who see themselves as the excluded. Those excluded from power between 1966 – 1992 appear to have learned no lessons about the necessity for partnership, democratic participation and inclusion.

Before continuing the historical trajectory of democracy in Guyana, it is worth setting down some markers of what it means for a system of government to be democratic. It should then be possible to examine the relationships between institutional demands and political behaviour and to identify the shortcomings. One can then proceed to examine what might be done to harmonise public philosophy, political behaviour and appropriate democratic institutions.

(4) Democratic Intent, Democratic Institutions, Undemocratic Politics.

In post independence Guyana, there has never been any public doubt that liberal representative democracy and its institutions provide the most desirable means for organising public life and making political decisions. Even the PPP in Marxist mode has never raised open questions about electoral democracy, while the PNC, at its dictatorial zenith, always operated behind a façade of democratic behaviour. It kept faith with regular elections, even while subverting them.

In fact, the 1966 draft constitution that the PNC government presented to the independence conference in London was more generous in its hopes and expectations (see its preamble for pledges about 'the nation' and the residence of 'power'), than the one finally agreed with the British government.

The Preamble to the 1966 (PNC) draft [15] stated:	The Preamble to the 1966 Guyana Independence Constitution stated that:
We, the people of Guyana – Believing that all men are entitled to certain fundamental and inalienable RIGHTS, among which are: JUSTICE, social, economic and political; LIBERTY of thought, expression, belief, faith and worship; EQUALITY of status and of opportunity before the law; and recognising the DUTY of all men to uphold and maintain these RIGHTS, to strive to promote the COMMON WEAL, To support and sustain the NATION, And to preserve its UNITY, INTEGRITY, and INDEPENDENCE; and Desiring to affirm that SOVEREIGN POWER resides with the PEOPLE – do DECLARE ourselves a NATION, and Accept and Adopt this CONSTITUTION.	Whereas the People of Guyana (a) acknowledge that reverence for the Deity and respect for the inherent dignity and the equal and inalienable rights of all men are the foundation of freedom, justice and peace in society; (b) affirm the entitlement of all men to the fundamental rights and freedoms of the individual; (c)recognise that the said rights and freedoms are best established in a democratic society founded upon the rule of law. Now therefore the following articles which make provision for the government of Guyana as such a democratic society, shall have effect on the Constitution of Guyana.

Having declared their resolve, the constitution makers set out to satisfy their aims by designing democratic institutions. That is they provided for:

(a) Public-decision making through elected representatives. Government and Opposition were enshrined.
(b) Regular, free, and fair elections. Periodic changes of government was assumed.
(c) The rule of law and an independent Judiciary.
(d) Access to information from a variety of sources.
(e) Freedom of association.
(f) Freedom of expression.
(g) Inclusive citizenship.[23]

The 1966 Guyana independence constitution followed the British interpretation of democracy closely but it was not an imposition. It came, with British consent, from the dominant section of the Guyanese elite whose open declaration was to transform a colonial expression into a functioning participative entity. In this they were in good company. In 1942 Schumpeter had defined democratic institutions as "arrangements for arriving at political decisions in which individuals acquire the power to decide by means of a competitive struggle for the people's vote".[24] Schumpeter's definition of democracy as a political method for arriving at legislative and administrative decisions can be enrolled in support of the view that, in polarised Guyana, democracy should not just be an end but a means to popular participation, cooperation, coexistence and growth of the notion of 'people'. In the conundrum of which comes first – Peace, Democracy or Development?[25] – this book argues for Democracy, Peace, Development in mutual modificatory tension.

This latter view was supported by the Prime Minister of Guiana at the opening session of the 1965 Constitutional Conference in London on 2 November 1965, when he said,[26]

More than symbolic of our conviction that the parliamentary opposition has a significant role to play, embodied in the draft constitution which the two parties in the government have brought with them, is a provision for the appointment of a leader of the opposition, consultation with whom on all important appointments will be obligatory. We also want to see in the constitution coming out of this conference, the institution of the office of Ombudsman, the holder of which will have statutory authority to investigate complaints of discrimination and irregular use of State-power,

and to take the necessary action in terms of the spirit of the
constitution and the public interest.

The draft constitution contains several provisions aimed at
ensuring the independence of the judiciary, and the enshrinement
of human rights, but it is not so much what is written in the
constitution as the spirit in which it is worked that counts. And
as we cut the political chains which have bound us to Britain in
the past, we take with us the legacy of the democratic concept
while we embark upon the building of a new nation – a nation
in which we hope to abolish poverty and unemployment, and
for the first time ensure the little man full participation in all
the affairs of the country and a recognition of his innate human
dignity.

And yet, the ink had barely dried on the constitution when
plans were afoot to subvert its provisions. To the PNC, coalition
government was humbug and had to be dismantled. By the
1968 elections, rigged use of overseas and proxy voting ensured
a working majority for the PNC. From hereon, until 1992,
every election was 'won' by the PNC with ever increasing
majorities as their rigging techniques became more elaborate
and brazen.[27] This not only flew in the face of the fundamental
requirement of 'free competition for a free vote,'[28] it also denied
that democracy is "a regime in which governmental offices
are filled as a result of contested elections. Only if the opposition
is allowed to compete, win and assume office is a regime
democratic."[29] So much for the Prime Minister's adherence
to the 'democratic concept'. This question of the periodic changes
of regime and its dilemmas in a sharply divided and unbalanced
polity will keep coming back in the arguments which follow.
It is being discussed here in relation to the existing definitions
which the country espoused then and continues to do now.

The flagrant disregard for electoral propriety through fic-
titiously expanded electoral rolls, enfranchisement of the dead,
disenfranchisement of the living and changing the contents
of ballot boxes among other vote-gathering techniques, is well
documented.[30] The paragraphs which follow illustrate the systematic destruction of the rule of law as provided for in the
constitution.

In the last election before independence (1964) the PNC
received 40.5% of the votes cast. The first since independence

(1968) brought them 56% in a situation where neither loyalties nor population distribution had changed.[31] They could now make changes to the constitution which only needed a simple majority.

The 1973 elections gave the Party 70.15% of the votes allegedly cast and meant that changes could now be made which required a two thirds majority.[32] The final hurdle for total 'party paramountcy' was the constitutional safeguard which demanded that certain fundamental rights could only be changed by a two-thirds majority and popular approval by referendum. The PNC sought to remedy this in 1978. Instead of general elections the country was asked to forego the need for a referendum in future changes. Despite massive opposition – it was estimated that 75% of the people were against such a drastic change – and an estimated 15% turn out, the government claimed that 70.5% of the electorate had voted. 97.4% of these were declared to have given approval for the change.[33]

With total control in their hands, the government set out to rewrite the constitution in its own socialist image. Replicated hereunder the aims were suitably high sounding and the social democratic institutions satisfied the earlier criteria impeccably.

THE 1980 CONSTITUTION OF THE COOPERATIVE REPUBLIC OF GUYANA PREAMBLE [34]

WE THE PEOPLE OF THE CO-OPERATIVE REPUBLIC OF GUYANA, the proud heirs of the indomitable spirit and unconquerable will of our forefathers who by their sacrifices, their blood and their labour made rich and fertile and bequeathed to us as our inalienable patrimony for all time this green land of Guyana;

SALUTING the epic struggles waged by our forefathers for freedom, justice and human dignity and their relentless hostility to imperialist and colonial domination and all other forms and manifestations of oppression;

ACCLAIMING   those immortal leaders who in the vanguard of battle kept aloft in the banner of freedom by the example of their courage, their fortitude and their martyrdom, whose names and deeds being forever enshrined in our hearts we forever respect, honour and revere;

INSPIRED   by the glorious victory of 26th May, 1966, when after centuries of heroic resistance and revolutionary endeavour we liberated ourselves from colonial bondage, won political independence and became free to mould our own destiny;

CONSCIOUS   of the fact that to bring about conditions necessary for the full flowering of the creative genius of the people of Guyana formal political sovereignty must be complemented by economic independence and cultural emancipation;

HAVING
ESTABLISHED   the Republic on 23rd February, 1970, to reinforce our determination to chart an independent course of development in conformity with our historical experience, our cultural heritage and our common aspirations;

PLEDGED   to defend our national sovereignty, to respect human dignity and to cherish and uphold the principles of freedom, equality and democracy and all other fundamental human rights;

DEDICATED   to the principle that the people of Guyana are entitled as of right to enjoy the highest possible standard of living and quality of life consistent with their work and the possibilities of the country's resources;

CONVINCED   that the organisation of the State and society on socialist principles is the only means of ensuring social and economic justice for all of the people of Guyana; and, therefore,

BEING MOTIVATED and guided by the principles of socialism;

BEING OPPOSED to all social, economic and political systems which permit the exploitation of man by man; and

ACKNOWLEDGING our common purpose of national cohesion and our common destiny as one people and one nation,

DO SOLEMNLY
RESOLVE to establish the State on foundations of social and economic justice, and accordingly by popular consensus, after full, free and open discussion, debate and participation,

DO ADOPT The following —

THE CONSTITUTION OF THE COOPERATIVE REPUBLIC OF GUYANA.

But rhetoric and the provision of democratic institutions are one thing, action and the practice of democratic politics are another. Without the latter, everything else is 'as sounding brass and a tinkling cymbal.'[35] With full control of the state and its organs, the PNC government continued to rig elections,[36] to use its power of patronage to dominate the public services, the police, the army[37] and the entire legal system.[38] By 1980 the public media – sound and print – were safely in the 'hands of the government.'[39] There was no television broadcasting. Those newspapers, such as the W.P.A.'s *Dayclean*, which defied manipulation and chose to offer dissenting opinions were strangled through the denial of newsprint and heavy fines by a compliant legal system. In such a system, the much vaunted sanctity of human rights were trampled on with impunity while trade unions who were not in the pockets of the government had to fight a continuous rearguard battle to maintain some semblance of independence.[40] The role of the Caribbean Conference of Churches newspaper, *Caribbean Con-*

tact, which operated from Trinidad under the editorship of the banned Guyanese journalist Rickey Singh, was one of the few sources of regular and reliable information. Opposition Parties were harassed relentlessly, their public meetings broken up and the assassination of the WPA's Walter Rodney was only one of a number of political murders.[41]

When President for life L F S Burnham died in 1985 and his deputy, Desmond Hoyte took over, an independent newspaper (*Stabroek News*) was allowed to function; fear and thuggery diminished, but not much else of democratic significance happened. In fact, those carefully crafted 1980 institutions continued to be mocked daily by lopsided and inept political behaviour from the very people who had declared them the peoples' constitution.[42]

So, having borrowed liberal democratic ideas from the colonialists as a bargaining chip for independence, the new Guyanese leaders also borrowed their ideas of how to govern. For colonial rule was never democratic. It followed Furnival's description of the colonial plural society where a minority took power and enforced it ruthlessly in the pursuit of social order. It is therefore not surprising that confronted with the problems of ethnicity and cultural diversity, the post-independence leaders instinctively turned to the centralisation of power, discouragement of opposition and meeting protest "with more highly tempered steel." Democratic institutions had met undemocratic politics and the whole country was diminished by the encounter.

By 1992 the Cold War had ended. Liberal democracy was deemed triumphant and Francis Fukuyama could declare 'the end of history.'[43] Electoral democracy, as against a declaration of anti-communism, was once again deemed the hallmark of good governance. Guyana too was liberated from the dead hand of American nightmares. In that year, under the watchful gaze of the conscience of America – ex-President Jimmy Carter – 'free and fair' elections were held. The PPP won. Its ethnic majority did not waver. Additionally it claimed a broader ethnic base with the addition of a Civic group drawn mainly from among the African Guyanese. For good measure, and whatever the dilutions within, the Leader reaffirmed publicly that the Party remained Marxist, though its policies continued the programme of economic liberalisation begun under Desmond Hoyte. As noted above, they won again in 1997 and in 2001. On 15 July 2003, the editor of the *Stabroek News* could write, "In Guyana today there is freedom of speech, freedom of assembly, freedom of movement, indeed a high degree of the traditional human rights. It is by most standards an open society."[44] Yet the main organ of liberal democracy – Parliament – which should "provide a forum for rational discussion of political problems and optimum settlement of different and potentially conflicting social interests",[45] does not work. Despite rewriting and amendments to its constitution, Parliament has not worked since independence. And this is regardless of whether membership has been determined by 'free and fair' or 'rigged' elections.

Why is this so?

According to the Guyanese themselves, politics in Guyana is driven by racial loyalties. This is kept tight by political entrepreneurs who base their appeal on the imagined excesses if the other side were to be allowed to win power.

These fears and resentments are openly supported by sections of the media who confuse liberation with license. They see the stifling of rational debate and the promotion of racial hatred as part of their contribution to instability and the promotion of change in favour of those whom they support.

The result is that those who win at elections are seen to have exclusive access to the resource and status allocations of the state while the losers see themselves as excluded from the benefits of citizenship.

Whether these claims and counter claims are true or not, Parliament ceases to be the forum for discussion, dissent and decision for which it is designed. Citizenship, whose principal task is to elect representatives to govern, is mocked when opposition is transferred to the street and every effort is made to demonstrate governmental incompetence and corruption, thereby generating instability, lack of confidence and economic stagnation. Electoral authority loses its legitimacy.

In this culture of total opposition, sabotage and violence against people and property are deemed acceptable political behaviour. The rule of law ceases to have meaning. It must be repeated that while their tactics might vary, the foregoing points are true of both the PPP/C and the PNC.

Something more sinister lurks in the shadowy background. It is the series of questions which ask:

Whose space is it anyway?

Is it, like the majority of the English-speaking Caribbean, an African space?

If so, how is the majority Indian population to be dealt with? By accommodation? Domination? Or ethnic cleansing by 'other means'?

The result is developmental stagnation and political deadlock. To continue the editorial quotation, "It [Guyana] is at the same time poor and underdeveloped. There is unemployment, illiteracy and a low standard of living. These problems affect the whole society, not one section of it."

In his Walter Rodney Memorial Lecture, 19 July 2002, David Hinds summed up the malady of Guyana during the preceding decade in the following words:

> When a political party, which is not a guerrilla movement, makes good on its pledge to make the country ungovernable, it is not only the patriotism of the party that must be questioned, but most importantly it is the political culture and the political system that must be seriously questioned. The government has struggled to stamp its authority, a situation that has hampered its ability to push through its programs and to maintain law and order...
>
> The workability of political systems is based in part on popular confidence... No one with any honesty can bear witness that our government enjoys popular multiracial confidence. There is, therefore, a serious political crisis in the country that paralyses the political institutions. In other words the already shaky institutions have collapsed under the weight of the political competition for power. This is a crisis of both legitimacy and confidence.[46]

So for 39 years parliamentary democracy, the system whereby elected representatives attempt to "govern in all public matters all of the time",[47] has served the Guyanese people disastrously. By all the canons of scientific inquiry the time has surely come for a radical reconstruction of some of our political institutions. It seems clear that the principles of winning and losing, government and opposition, which are the current institutional bedrock, are totally unsuitable for a deeply divided society in which one side has a permanent majority. Exclusion (real or imagined) eventually encourages the growth of insecurity, denies participation, invites the humiliation of misrecognised identity, breeds distributive injustice and undermines the ability of citizens to influence important aspects of their lives. These are human existential needs and will always be pursued. If they are denied satisfaction, violence is the inevitable end.

The way forward, it has been argued elsewhere,[48] is for the Guyanese to fundamentally rethink the needs of their multi-ethnic society in mediated, collaborative dialogue and in the light of these deliberations to redesign their institutions and practices which will satisfy the common human existential needs of all their people. This book will concentrate on making the case for fully participative democratic institutions, both at the local or national levels, as the means to satisfy those needs. It will argue for the expunging of ideas about winning and losing, government and opposition, (in the adversarial mode as we know them now) from the Guyanese political vocabulary and their replacement with thoughts and practices based on sharing, participation, and citizenship. It will set out to fuse ideas, institutions and action so that participation might grow, insecurity might diminish, trust might be restored and we might begin to build decency into our society. In more formal terms, the hypothesis which guides the book is:

- That democracy for Guyana must provide for representatives of all the people, at both national and local levels, to govern in all their interests all of the time,
- That democratic institutions and democratic politics must seek to give meaning to the country's proclamation as a cooperative republic through an actively engaged citizenry all of the time.

The thoughts presented here are not meant to be a blueprint. There is no blueprint. Rather, they are a contribution to that serious debate which must take place if Guyanese are to create conditions for living in a state of acceptable social justice and peaceful coexistence. The next chapter will examine the arguments for participation and its role in the development of responsible citizenship and growth of 'the people'. This is an important end for the democratic process in a multi-ethnic state if democracy is to become self sustaining and able to confront its social and economic problems and resolve its conflicts.

END NOTES

1. Williams, E. (1944), *Capitalism and Slavery,* North Carolina, Chapel Hill, p. 98.
2. Soon after it came to power in 1992, the Leader of the PPP declared that the Party remained true to its Marxist beliefs. This was probably more for international rather than domestic consumption. The New World Group had recognised as far back as 1964 that the PPP had always been an alliance of bureaucratic Stalinists, romantic revolutionaries, socialists, trade unionists, small business people and generally unideological members of the urban and rural working classes and semi-peasantry. After the split, the non-Marxist ethnic elements came to play a much more influential role. See *New World Quarterly, Guyana Independence Issue*, David De Caires and Miles Fitzpatrick, 'Twenty Years of Politics in Our Land', pp. 39-45.
3. With the addition of a Civic section to the Government (whose members are mainly African Guyanese politicians without any significant political constituency), the PPP claims a broader inter-ethnic base and therefore greater ethnic legitimacy.
4. For a detailed analysis of the events surrounding the Georgetown gaol-break and the events in Buxton in 2001-2002, see Frederick Kissoon, 'The Failure of the Buxton Conspiracy', originally published in the *Chronicle* and *Kaietur News* papers in June 2002, and posted on the Guyana undersiege website, May 2002. (http;//www. guyana undersiege.com/ROAR/FK%20Buxton %20Conspiracy.htm)
5. See UNHCR, Guyana: Criminal Violence and Police Response, GUY100762.E , 2004. (http://www.unhcr.org/ refworld/country,,,,GUY,4562d94e2,45f1473f29,0.html). This article has a detailed listing of relevant articles in the Guyanese press.
6. See Gordon French, 'UN committee urges prompt inquiries into alleged extra-judicial killings in Guyana', Caribbeannet News, November 28, 2006 (www.caribbeannetnews.com/cgi-script/csArticles/articles/000044/004449.htm). And see Tristram Korten, 'Gang's terror reign in Guyana years in making', *The*

Miami Herald, 16 June 2008, available on the Pulitzer Centre for Crisis Reporting Website (Centrewww.pulitzercenter.org/openitem.cfm?id=919)

7. Identifiable, that is, by ethnic bonds of "language, religion, race, homeland, customs, ancestry, etc.... and shared by the Sikhs, the Tamils, Malays, Yorubas, Jews, Basque, Kurds, Palestinians, etc.." See Premdas, R. R. (1997), *Ethnicity and the Anatomy of Ethnic Conflicts in the World Today*, U.W.I., Trinidad, Institute of International Relations, pp. 4-5.

8. Seecoomar, J. (2002), *Contributions Towards The Resolution Of Conflict in Guyana*, Leeds, Peepal Tree Press.

9. Ibid., Chap. Six.

10. One should except from this general criticism the poet Martin Carter, who even while still a member of the PPP wrote of the dangers of ethnic fragmentation and the failure of a class-oriented Marxist analysis of Guyana's social forces to address ethnicity as a serious threat to social order. (See Martin Carter, Leader, *Thunder*, 5 March 1955; and 'The Racists Among Us', *Thunder*, 24 Sept. 1955.) Another early critique of the assumptions that there had once been an ethnically harmonious politics before the Jagan/Burnham split is to be found in the Special Guyana edition of *New World Quarterly*; see note 2 above.

11. See for instance Tacuma Ogunseye in *Stabroek News*, Sept 5, 2008. Referring to one of the leaders of a gang who was quite probably responsible for two mass killings in Guyana in 2008, Ogunseye wrote: "Finally, I want to say that my assessment of the situation leads me to the position that Rawlins and his comrades were engaged in a political struggle. They were not criminals in the ordinary sense even though they may have committed crimes for both political and personal reasons. Fineman and his comrades were African Resistance Fighters and they had their strengths and weaknesses – after all, they were only human."

12. See page 9 of *Contributions Towards The Resolution...*

13. Adapted from Nath,D. (1970), *A History of Indians in Guiana*, London (np), p. 236.

14. www.guyana.org/ *The Guyana Worldwide Year Handbook: Facts At a Glance.*

15. See Guyana News and Information: 'Past election results'. (www.guyana.org/Elections/past_results.html)

16. CO.(1951) *British Guiana Report of the Constitutional Commission 1950-51,* p 22, London, HMSO.

17. Shahabuddeen, M. (1978), *Constitutional Development in Guyana 1621 – 1978,* p. 535, Georgetown.

18. Ibid., p. 536

19. See the recently published Stephen G. Rabe, *U.S. Intervention in British Guiana: A Cold War Story* (University of North Carolina Press, 2005) which sets out very clearly, on the basis on newly released CIA documents just how implicated that organisation was in making use of racial violence to destabilise the Jagan government.

20. Lewis, W. A. (1965), *Politics in West Africa,* p. London, Allen and Unwin.

21. Cooper, R, (2002), 'The new liberal imperialism', *The Observer,* London, 7.4.2002./ Special Reports; Thomas, C.Y. (2003), 'The failed state dilemma' *Stabroek News,* Georgetown, 6.7.2003; and Russell, B. (2003), 'World leaders reject Blair's move over military action' *The Independent',* London, 15.7.2003.

22. *Proposed Draft of the Constitution of Guyana, (nd.),* Government Printing and Stationery Office, Georgetown, British Guiana.

23. Statutory Instruments, 1966.

24. Schumpeter,J, (1942), *Capitalism, Socialism and Democracy,* New York, Harper, p. 242.

25. Both McDonald, G. M. ((1998), 'Alternative Perspectives in   Peace Building in Columbia and El Salvador', Unpublished PhD dissertation, University Of Bradford, p. 80) and Azar, E.E. (1986) ('Protracted International Conflicts: Ten Propositions' in Burton, J. and Dukes, F., (1990), *Conflict: Readings in Management and Resolution,* London, Macmillan, p. 155) have   posed Peace and Development. I have added Democracy because I am arguing that Democracy is peacemaking and development in action.

26. Burnham, F. (1970), *A Destiny To Mould*, New York, Africana Publishing Corporation, pp. 112-113.

27. For a more detailed description of electoral manipulation, see my (2002). Contributions *Towards The Resolution of Conflict*

in Guyana, Leeds, Peepal Tree Press, Chap,4. In fact this section takes its evidence from the research done for this chapter.

28. Schumpeter, J. (1942), p.217.
29. Przeworski, A. et al. (1996), 'What makes Democracies Endure?' in *Journal of Democracy, Vol.* 7 No 1 pp. 50-51.
30. Thomas, C.Y. (1983), 'State Capitalism in Guyana', in Ambursely, F. and Cohen, R. eds., *Crisis in the Caribbean,* NY. Monthly Review Press, p.37; and Chase, A. (1994), *Guyana, A Nation In Transit, Burnham's Role,* Georgetown, Guyana, Pavnikpress, pp. 25-29; and Ferguson, T. (1999), *To Survive Sensibly or to Court Heroic Death. Management of Guyana's Political Economy, 1965-1985,* Georgetown, Guyana, National Printers Ltd., p.29; and Spinner, T. J. (1984), *A Political And Social History Of Guyana, 1945-1983,* London, Westview, pp. 145-146.
31. Spinner, T. J. (1984), p. 127
32. Ibid., p. 146.
33. Ibid., pp. 164 –167.
34. Charter 88 Unlocking Democracy, www.charter88.org.uk
35. The Holy Bible, 1 Corinthians: Chap.13, V. 1.
36. Latin American Bureau, (1984), *Guyana: Fraudulent Revolution,* London, LAB, pp. 41-42. And see Morrison, A. (1998), *Justice: The Struggle for Democracy in Guyana, 1952-1992.* Georgetown, Red Thread Women's Press, pp. 334-5.
37. Danns, G. K. (1982), *Domination and Power in Guyana,* London, Transaction Books, pp. 174-6.
38. Guyana Human Rights Association, (1981), *Human Rights Report,* Georgetown, pp. 21-22; and Caribbean Conference of Churches, (1991), 'Official Report of A Goodwill And Fact-finding Mission To Guyana, Sept.-Oct. 1990,' Bridgetown, Barbados, pp. 31-32.
39. Premdas, R. R. (1995), *Ethnic Conflict and Development: The Case Of Guyana,* Aldershot, Avebury, pp. 136-137; GHRA (1981), p.28.
40. Morrison, A. (1998), pp. 356-361.
41. Ibid., pp. 130-167.
42. See *What The People's New Constitution Means To You,* (1980) Guyana, Ministry of Information

43. Fukuyama, F. (1989), 'The End of History?' *The National Interest,* 16: 3-18.

44. www.stabroeknews.com/editorial, 15 July 2003.

45. Hinds, D. (2002), *Race, Democracy, And Power Sharing,* www.guyanacaribbeanpolitics.com

46. Ibid.

47. Barber, B.R. (1984), *Strong Democracy: Participatory Politics for a New Age,* London, University of California Press, p. xiv.

48. Seecoomar, J. (2002), Chap. 7 and Appendix One of this book.

CHAPTER TWO.

LOCAL GOVERNMENT: THE LINCHPIN FOR GUYANESE DEMOCRACY.

We affirm that nations cannot be built without the popular support and full participation of people, nor can economic crisis be resolved and the human and economic conditions improved without the full and effective contribution, creativity and political enthusiasm of the majority of people. We believe strongly that popular participation, in essence [is] the empowerment of people to effectively involve themselves in creating the structures and in designing policies and programmes, that serve the interest of all, as well as to effectively contribute to the development process and share equitably in its benefits. Therefore, there must be an opening up of political processes to accommodate freedom of opinions, tolerate differences, accept consensus on issues, as well as ensure the effective participation of people and their organisation and association.
(International Conference on Popular Participation in the Recovery and Development Process in Africa, 1990.)[1]

As a goal of social and political organisation, the Lincolnesque ideal of democracy as "government of the people, by the people, for the people" is now, in form at least, "the pre-eminently acceptable form of governance."[2] It has not always been so. Autocracy has hitherto held that pride of place. In fact, liberal democracy is one of the outstanding bequests of the twentieth century. That it might not be finally realisable as a form of government, and more so, in a multi-ethnic state, is not the question here. What is at stake is how we arrange ourselves so that our existential need to belong and participate can be given satisfactory rein and without recourse to violence. So for us, to continue the engineering metaphor, democracy is the system of roads we build and upon which we travel towards the good society. We *might* never get there, but so long as the peoples are fully engaged in the construction and the journey, approximations will do. They will do as long as they are not permanent and continuing collaborative efforts are made to push towards new and better approximations. Out of this action might come a working consensus, legitimacy and "the people" side by side with the "peoples". It is a long term political activity. In Guyana, the first 39 years of independence have been wasted through ethnic infighting over which group is to control the state, its resource and status distributions. Out of this has come continuing political instability, social decay and economic stagnation.

In these circumstances one is led to ask – Is democracy possible in a multi-ethnic society after the age of external domination? In 1861, John Stuart Mill[3] thought not. In his own words:

> Free institutions are next to impossible in a country made up of different nationalities. Among a people without fellow feeling, especially if they read and speak different languages, the united opinion necessary to the working of representative government, cannot exist.

One hundred years on, Rambushka and Shepsle,[4] on the basis of more detailed empirical evidence, came to the same conclusion. For them, there seems to be no workable way out of an entrepreneurial leadership, rooted in ethnicity and prepared to go to any lengths to gain or maintain control of the state and its resources. In such circumstances the future is civil war and its brutalities – genocide, ethnic cleansing, defeat and domination.

But amid this democratic wilderness not all Guyanese have fallen in love with anarchy and lawlessness. There are voices across the divide which speak unrelentingly of the good society and how it might be achieved. Much of this is based on the work of Eusi Kwayana,[5] Arthur Lewis,[6] Arend Lijphart[7] and their followers who argue for a power sharing approach to democratic governance as a means to reconcile diversity, encourage consensus on a minimum set of values and promote political stability. Their ideas and thoughts on what this means will be given prominence later on. For now, however, the focus will be on some of the universal requirements of democracy, their shortfalls in states dominated by ethnic politics and how these fissiparous urges might be countered. How, in other words, a voting democracy might be transformed into a working democracy.[8]

According to Charles Taylor,[9] if a democratic society is to function effectively, its minimum requirements are:

- Firstly, a unity of purpose among its people. This does not mean total agreement but a set of common goals which provide a focus for open debate and considered choice.
- Secondly, it requires that its citizens are treated equally, and
- Thirdly, that the society is prepared to deliver on its obligations to its members.

These are minimum conditions of legitimacy which belong to a democratic society. They are not negotiable.

In most of the post 1950s multi-ethnic societies and Guyana in particular, there are 'peoples' but no 'people'. There are identity group struggles for control but no common goals. Notions of equality are mouthed but are not real and paralysis, not progress, prevails. Instead of the dynamic of inclusive dialogue there is simmering discontent in separate corners. In this void, violence emerges as the logical means to break the deadlock. The welfare of the people is but an illusion.

This book will argue that the key to the development of common goals, a common political will, equality and welfare satisfaction, is participation. In short, the maximum possible participation in decision making is the key to the development of 'the people'. Put more dogmatically, there can be no democracy, no peace, no 'people' without the fullest possible involvement of all groups and their representatives in the development of policy and of action.

The next section will deal with some theoretical considerations concerning participation and cooperation. It represents a free ranging adaptation of the work of David Mitrany (1966), and his colleagues, which dealt largely with functional cooperation as a *Working Peace System,* for postwar international relations.

1. Functional Cooperation

In his article on global governance which was published in the April 2003 issue of *Round Table*, Sir Shridath Ramphal quoted Barbara Ward with approval. Years ago, the noted social scientist had said, "We are either going to be a community or we are going to die."[10] The argument which runs throughout this book is that community is the proper end state of democracy. It is recognisable when common values, attitudes, beliefs and loyalties begin to take root and guide actions in the society. It is not attainable through a process of spontaneous generation nor can it be wished into existence. It will happen, if it happens at all, through institutions which include all and encourage continuous and unrelenting hard work because real benefits are seen to accrue to all. The challenge of achieving this is magnified several times over and becomes more urgent when the staring point is ethnic infighting.

Functional cooperation is put forward here as one strategy towards the integrative process of developing a Guyanese community. It is the process whereby citizens learn through the opportunities provided for cooperation that their welfare needs could be satisfied more effectively through combined efforts than by obstruction. If this cooperative ethos is to take root and grow, particularly in a multi-ethnic society with narrowly defined and competing interests, the institutions for cooperation must be able to recognise, reconcile and satisfy these different interests quickly.[11] It is the price to be paid for the transference of loyalty from the parochial to the communal. It is also the basis for the legitimacy of authority at any level of social organisation.

Before continuing with the theoretical arguments for functional cooperation, let me hasten to illustrate what I have in mind as the most basic level of social organisation. Imagine, if you will, the village as the smallest unit of local administration. Councillors are elected by popular vote after due process of campaigning and public debate. Funding is by local taxation and central government subvention. Councillors are accountable to their village electorate for expenditure, its achievements and failures. Free and fair elections are held at regular intervals and representatives can be changed or retained as the electorate decides. This is the involvement of villagers in their own affairs. Replicated throughout the country it gives meaning to the claim that democracy should provide opportunities for the revitalising of citizenship by encouraging all of the people to govern themselves in some public matters at least some of the time.[12]

2. Local Government in Guyana: the Background

However, before expanding on these ideas for nation-building at the local level, it is worth stepping back to look at the reality of the place of local government in the making of Guyana. My view, looking at the history, is that is an idea that has never been given the chance to flourish, a story of thwarted desires, spirit-sapping obstacles and a tendency amongst both colonial and postcolonial rulers to impose centralised 'solutions' that have failed to work.

The origins of governance at village level lay in the desire of African and Indian Guyanese to establish free settlements away from the authoritarian structures of the sugar estates. With the exception of some of the villages based on rice production in the Corentyne, the endemic problem of virtually all villages was poverty, an inability to escape from the economic orbit of the estates, the special Guyanese problem of the cost of drainage, and contradictory and shortsighted policies implemented by colonial governments. At the core of colonial policy, right into the twentieth century, was a half-heartedness about committing to real independence for the villages; the needs of the sugar estates for seasonal labour always remained paramount. And when there was a recognition that something needed to be done about the condition of roads through the villages or the unsanitary condition of many villages because of poor drainage, there was a reluctance to make the kind of investment that would have made a difference. When investment was made, for instance to carry out drainage projects using steam machinery, the colonial authorities tried to recover costs through rates set at levels that many villagers could not afford. Whilst several free villages were found to have independently provided themselves with an overseer and watchman by the 1860s, when central government imposed a system of overseers on all incorporated villages, the costs of the post frequently swallowed all the rate levied. Again, whilst the practice of providing labour for village projects was a reported feature of village life, when central government made payment for road maintenance or drainage projects compulsory, much resentment was engendered.[13]

Though there were at least a couple of Governors who appear to have paid more than lip-service to the problems of the villages (Governor Irving from 1882-1887 and Gormanston in 1892) central government was frequently confused in its administration, such as running a competing Board of Villages and Board of Health with overlapping powers, and introducing frequent new ordinances throughout the nineteenth century that tinkered with the system without addressing the villages' real needs. The constant, though, was the tendency to centralise and there was regular conflict between the tax-gathering ambitions of central government and impoverished villagers. As the Government Secretary noted in a Memorandum in 1903, the government had been forced to write off $75,000 of bad debt from just three villages.[14]

Whilst lip-service was paid to the principle of representation, there was evidently some reluctance on the part of villagers to engage in electing Councillors, quite probably since the whole apparatus was seen as imposed by the colonial government.

Some fifty years later, the Robertson Commission Report (1954) was damning in its assessment of the role of local government in the colonial administration. Paragraph 46 is worth quoting in full:

> In contradiction of the impression made upon the Waddington
> Commission by the system of local government we do not think
> that local government bodies play an important part in the affairs
> of British Guiana, and indeed we were not convinced that in local
> affairs the village and country district councils were popular or
> influential amongst the people. Their ineffectiveness seems to
> be mainly due to the facts that local government has little financial
> power and that its statutory functions are severely limited. A few
> councils, blessed with Chairmen of personality or energetic overseers,
> appear to play a part in community life, but in the great majority
> of cases the councils lack drive and influence; and even had they
> these qualities, it is doubtful if they could play a great part in
> affairs. Their only powers amount to their having some (but not
> all) responsibility for local drainage and irrigation and for maintaining
> local roads, for which they are authorised to raise local rates. It
> is true that there is voluntary association of local authorities into
> "Unions ", but these depend very much on individual enthusiasm
> and personality, and they lack any formal basis. The whole scope
> of local government, therefore, appears to be very limited. [15]

The Commission's statistic that the revenue of the then 43
village districts and 49 country districts amounted in 1952 to
£126,000, whilst expenditure amounted to only £121,000
indicated just why villagers would have regarded local government
as predominantly as system of taxation.[16]

Just a few years earlier (1951-2), when a young R.T. Smith
began ethnographic research in the African Guyanese village
of Hopetown (located between Mahaica and Berbice), his
observations provide both support for and further explanation
of what the Robertson Commission reported – though Hopetown
was particularly famed for "poor local government and delinquent
taxes". What Smith found was the same institution of village
overseer, "the classic village headman, caught between his
superiors in the central colonial government and his friends
and kin in the village".[17] He also found that the bugbears of
poverty and flood were no less endemic for many of the villagers
in 1951 as Government Secretary Ashmore had found, writing
in 1903. But what R.T. Smith also saw was that the tension
between local and central government had its ramifications
in the class and cultural stratification of the village itself. In
addition to the village overseer, there was also a village chairman,
who in the case of Hopetown was also a nominated member

of the Legislative Council, who in reality represented the village elite, a group defined by their access to colonial education. In Hopetown the chairman was the retired headmaster of the village school. In cultural terms this elite distinguished itself from the masses by its condemnation and avoidance of what was African-derived in African Guyanese culture such as Que-Que wedding celebrations, wakes and spirit possession. Without spelling it out, what Smith sees is an elite bound in to the centralising colonial order, and a rank and file suspicious and resistant to its authority.

What could have changed this was the impact of the independence movement and the prospect of the limited forms of self-government on offer in 1953, but then so rapidly withdrawn. R.T. Smith records how a Hopetown Discussion Group was formed, how it set up various committees to explore the possibilities of setting up a rice-farming co-operative, encouraging local industries and dealing with the perennial issues of health, drainage and irrigation and education. Smith records that the Discussion Group broke up over issues of "status, education and perceptions of competence".[18]

Yet as other accounts suggest, the onset of nationalist politics, and particularly the campaigning role of the PPP, began to wake the village populations from colonial slumber. But it is also apparent, that the new politics reinforced the centralising process by seeing the villages as vote banks for a Georgetown-based politics and not as places where Guyanese could develop their own localities.

Whilst it is a work of fiction with no pretence to sociological exactness, there is much in Jan Shinebourne's novel, *The Last English Plantation* (1987)[19] which is persuasive as a nuanced portrayal of the village world away from Georgetown. Set in the late 1950s in Berbice, the novel portrays both the sense of change within the village world and the way what was local to that world, though stimulated by the new politics, was also being swept away by its centralising force. (The novel also makes the point that whilst Old Dam, from which the main characters have moved, had a mixed African-Indian population, New Dam to which they move, a new extra-nuclear settlement of people who once lived on the sugar estate, is almost totally Indian.) The novel begins with an argument between Boysie Ramkarran, the local labour leader and Cyrus Lehall, a self-employed mechanic. It is about the perennial issue of weeding the drainage canals that run through the village. Cyrus is all for organising villagers to do the work; Boysie is adamant that it is the estate's responsibility. The argument reveals two things: the long-standing conflict repeated all over Guyana, between the interests of villages and the estates, and a shift in the power structure in the village. Once status had rested with people like Cyrus or old-timers like William Easen, who is an enthusiast for "a good village council" as a means of developing a region made backward by the power of the sugar estates, but now influence seems to rest with people like Boysie as a local representative of trade union power stimulated by the activities of the PPP. But this, too, is an illusion, as the climax of the novel reveals. Bidding to resolve a conflict within the village Easen says, "We are a community, and that is where you have to have agreement before the law can come into effect", but as police Sergeant Richards, with the power of his gun, dismissively reposts, "Let me tell you," the sergeant said, pointing north, "That is where the law made, Georgetown, by the leaders of this country". And the villagers remark ruefully how even their own man, Cheddi Jagan, though "once a sugar estate lad, had gone away and learnt his politics from books, while they had grown into big men on the estate and learnt their politics the hard way."[20] Whilst the newer villages that had grown as extra-nuclear settlements from the sugar estates differed in significant ways from the long-established independent villages,[21] both were swept up in the urge to centralise power.

Later, as African and Indian Guyanese began to perceive the world as being governed by us or by them, the villages themselves became the sites for divisive interests. During the years of the two Jagan pre-independence governments (1957-1961; 1961-1964), most Afro-Guyanese were absolutely certain that Indian villages received preferential treatment in terms of investment in agriculture. During the PNC years (1964-1992) the reverse was true, and though in the end all Guyanese suffered, visitors to the country during the later 1970s and 80s, often had no difficulty in distinguishing which were Afro- and which were Indo-Guyanese villages purely by the state of the roads.

Local representation through the electoral process was, indeed, another of the democratic deficits of the PNC years. After the rigged national elections of 1968, the PNC government went to especial lengths to ensure that the next local government elections, which were deferred until 1970, rigorously excluded the PPP opposition from the possibility of local power. Under any fair electoral system, the PPP would have undoubtedly won in at least two districts out of five (the PNC had split the elections into two rounds). By a crude mixture of voter list padding, gerrymandering of boundaries, proxy voting and ballot-box tampering, the PNC ensured that it won in all areas. The PPP withdrew in disgust from the second round of voting. These were the last local elections to be held until 1994.[22]

In 1980, the PNC introduced its co-operative constitution and reorganised the country into 10 administrative regions each of which were supposed to elect councillors to a National Congress of Local Democratic organs. In practice most councillors were PNC appointees, and in the 1985 regional elections the PNC 'won' all the seats.[23]

There were free municipal and local government elections in 1994 and these illustrated the capacity of a local electoral system to work as a counterbalance to the tendency of the majority ethnic group to permanent victory in the national elections. Although the PPP/C won 49 out of 71 council seats up for election, the success of the Good and Green Party (led by Hamilton Green, who had recently been expelled from the PNC) in winning the Georgetown municipality elections on the basis of working class Afro-Guyanese support, showed the potential for local and ethnically representative control.[24]

However, since 1994 there have been no further local government elections, and for this both the PPP/C and PNCR must share responsibility. Despite the establishment of the Guyana Elections Commission in 2000, and the fact that the need to reform the local government system formed part of the agreement made between President Bharrat Jagdeo and the new leader of the PNC, Robin Corbin, (following the death of Desmond Hoyte) no real progress has been made. For instance, local elections planned for 2004 did not take place because no agreement could be reached on the voters lists.

The relationship between central and local government has been no more positive in its contribution to healing ethnic divisions. Although there have been some impressive improvements to the country's transport infrastructure in road and bridge-building programmes, any visitor to Georgetown over the past decade will attest to the continuing sad decline of what was once known as the 'garden city' of the Caribbean, into a rubbish-strewn, pot-holed, poorly-drained ghost of itself. Whilst on occasions central government has bailed out the budget of the Georgetown municipality,[25] one must question whether the fact that the municipal council is evidently kept starved of resources is related to the fact that the PPP/C does not control the council. Whatever the reason, it offers another hostage to the accusations of ethnic bias in the distribution of resources.

3. Whither? What can local governance offer the democratic process and inter-ethnic relations?

It is only too evident from this brief review of the history of local government institutions and practice in Guyana that the principle of local democracy has never been given the chance to work. Whether at the hands of the colonial rulers up to the mid 20th century, or Guyana's post colonial rulers since 1966, the urge to control all power and resources centrally has vitiated the potential of decentralisation to offer the kind of local control that would offer all communities the feeling that they had a real stake in the decisions that controlled their lives. The balance between central and local government in democracies such as the United Kingdom is undoubtedly one of the factors contributing to political stability, where local councils are frequently led by political parties other than the party that controls central government, and where political independents outside the party system, representing specific local interests, have a much greater chance of election. In an ethnic mosaic such as Guyana, the principle of genuine local representation would require central government to accept not only the ceding of real power to local councils, but accepting partnerships across ethnic boundaries. The history with respect to the main political parties and their centralising urge is not positive, but the counter-evidence that Guyanese of all ethnicities 'get along' at the local level offers room for hope.

What I offer now is are some thoughts about how a devolved system of local government might work.

Imagine that the village is given responsibility for managing its own education, health, drainage and irrigation, roads, sanitation and local economic development among other welfare needs. Now take that perennial bugbear of Guyana's rural development – the flood – after any significant amount of rainfall. In order for Buxton or any other village to cope with the rainfall/drainage problem, its trenches, canals and 'kokers' have to be unblocked and free running. Now assume that neighbouring Annandale is less efficient, then Buxton's free running drains mean nothing. Annandale's floodwater would overflow into Buxton and both villages would suffer the ravages of flooding – lost crops, dead livestock and mosquitoes, overflowing latrines and other health hazards.

At some stage it could occur to the villagers and their leaders that there is a common problem which could be solved through discussion and a pooling of resources and from which all might benefit. Informal contacts might lead to the establishment of a joint flood committee with regular scheduled meetings to deal collaboratively with something which is beyond the capability of one village. Soon, also, the realisation might dawn on the new committee that the unit for flood control is too small and Friendship and Lusignan might be encouraged to see the good sense in joining to present a common front to a natural enemy. Anyone who has seen the pollution and rubbish clogging up the drainage canals along the East Coast Demerara road will recognise that involving the village communities in managing their own environment cannot come too soon.

A similar set of events could be imagined for any of the other areas of concern in village affairs. Take education. It goes without question that each village should manage its own primary provision. Secondary education, however, with its broader curriculum and more specialised needs, demands the kind of resource allocation which is likely to be beyond the means of one village but certainly within the reach of two. In our four village scenario, it would be natural for Buxton and Friendship to organise one secondary unit while Annandale and Lusignan organise the other. But secondary education has its own set of professional challenges and there would be everything to gain if regular meetings took place between the two sets of professionals who shared the challenges, experience and expertise in the education of adolescents. But there is more. Education is the linchpin of development and so the need for local tertiary education will have to be faced. This is far too expensive for one or two to contemplate. Our four village consortium, accustomed to some degree of cooperation, might well be the logical service provider.

The illustration of functional cooperation given above is deliberately painted in broad strokes. It is based on the following assumptions:

- That local communities should have the responsibility to govern themselves in matters which concern their welfare.
- That where problems are beyond the capacity of one village to solve, cooperation with neighbours should be sought and encouraged.
- That where technical expertise (including financial) to solve local problems is unavailable, this should be freely available as central government aid. Central government should be an enabler not a controller.
- That some problems are so widespread that an ever increasing number of village units would recognise the need to cooperate if the problems are to be solved.
- This is organic growth through functional necessity and voluntarily entered into. It is not bureaucratic imposition. The outcome of this natural growth

might very well become the region but it will be a region of the people's choice. Form, should follow function, and not vice versa.

- It is this ever increasing number of crosscutting and enmeshing circles of relationships which will encourage the growth of cooperation, trust, common welfare values, and the gradual emergence of understanding, commitment and of a Guyanese people.

- In other words this collaborative approach to welfare problems, assisted by technical support, becomes a real possibility for human governance in a divided state.

- At this level, the conundrum of which comes first – peace or development? – becomes irrelevant. The answer is neither – they go hand in hand.

But theoretical propositions are not enough. As part of an earlier research project, Guyanese respondents, asked the question about what should be done to make the country a better place in which to live, had this to say:

> ...I would start with a serious look at the devolution of power using the three counties as administrative units. Shove power away from the centre. One of the chief problems of Guyana is this whole business of the ferocity of the competition for central power. If you devolve power as much as you could within the country, you wouldn't have this craving, this thirst for power at the centre. This would accommodate peoples' drives for public office. There is too much power concentrated at the centre.
>
> People need to be involved in decision making. No one in Corriverton or Anna Regina or Pomeroon must have to come to Georgetown to appeal to somebody for administrative justice. No one should have to be traipsing up and bloody down for things which could be easily done in the regions. It is unfair. People need to be able to hold a local politician right there in Anna Regina or Pomeroon or wherever and throttle him if he doesn't deliver. There must be local accountability. If this society is to be saved, there must be devolution of power and responsibility.
>
> Dougla Guyanese.

…Community development systems which were destroyed in order to control have to be weaned back. They can't be put back overnight. For instance, in a village, the Chairman was known to the villagers. He became Chairman because he was respected. The villagers related to him and they did so with all the councillors. His race did not matter. He represented everybody. Now that system was destroyed and the whole country was divided into 10 amorphous Regions with leaders foisted on the people. That is an area which has to be worked at.

Local community structures have to be developed and put in place. When we were given Proportional Representation that local accountability was removed both for Local Government and for Parliament. Once you remove accountability from a system it is almost bound to collapse. I have no Councillor whom I have elected for my ward. If I want something done, I have to find a willing listener, go through the process of begging for a favour and 'greasing' a palm. In such a case, my natural inclination is to seek an ally of similar background to me. I go and try to find a 'Putagee man.' Someone else seeks out a Black man and so on. It is natural that in any situation of insecurity, you go and seek out your own kind and this reinforces racial behaviour.

Portuguese Guyanese.

The Touchau is the leader of the village. Whenever there is something to be done, he would call a meeting and the whole village would turn out. They would give their views. They would then decide and set a date. This includes the women too. On the day that they agreed, everybody would turn up to do the work. It is compulsory, even if someone has other things to do. It is like self help. The Touchau supervises to make sure it is done properly.

Amerindian Guyanese.

My feelings are that fear and suspicion are created by the politics of the land. Politicians have got to be large enough to rule this country so that all the people would believe that they are nationals rather than partisans. Attitudes have to change but I think other efforts have to be made to bring this about rather than wait on time alone to make it happen. Somehow we have to have a sharing of power and I mean not only political power but social and economic power also. I am not sure about how the political bit can be done but I think the whole country has to debate it…

But let us take Region Two and economic power. The region is largely rice growing and Indians are the main rice farmers. That does not mean that others should be shut out of it and other forms of agri-based development. Mechanisms must be put in place for other aspects – fruit, coconut, ground provision farming, fishing and shrimping. You know there is now growing worldwide demand for organic produce. Small businesses and cooperatives must be encouraged to take part…

Our system of Proportional Representation can keep us divided. We don't have constituency representatives and so we have to turn to someone of the same race to look after our interests. It is the same thing in the villages. We need our own village councillors. Development should start at the grass roots and they should be able to help the villagers discuss, decide, and start up local businesses. The cooperatives should be looked at again and regenerated especially at the village level.

Dartmouth and Better Success are neighbouring villages. One is Black and the other Indian. They do not wake up every morning with plans to burn each other's houses down. They are good neighbours. In times of trouble they look after one another. Some love, marry and have children together. With help and encouragement and leadership they should be able to take that start to a higher level...

Indian Guyanese.

We must go back to the village. Our ancestors wanted to live in villages and wanted to organise and run them for their own benefit. They were prevented from doing this both before independence and after independence. The big regions don't work for us. Only those who get employment from them have a good word to say for them. Why should I pay taxes without having a say in how dem spen de money and wha dem spend it on.

I have no councillor to protect my rights or to complain to. This region thing don't work. I want to have a say about what has to be done in my village so that all the villagers can get some benefit from the taxes we pay. No one takes any pride in the village anymore. We want our pride and our rights back.

African Guyanese.

This last quotation sums up the history[26] and current state of Guyanese local government with precision and great feeling It needs no attempt to clarify or paraphrase. The other respondents argued for:

- the devolution of power to the people so that they might be able to take part in making those decisions which affect their lives,
- the restoration of local community structures which allowed for elected councillors and so for intimacy and accountability. There was general hostility to the division of the country into 10 amorphous regions with leaders foisted on the people. It was felt that this made only for

continuing central control and no effective local
participation,
- as in the Amerindian villages, if local control is returned
  to the coastal villages, self help and cooperation might
  be encouraged,
- development to begin at the grass roots. Small businesses
  and cooperatives could be encouraged in fruit, coconut,
  ground provision farming, fishing, shrimping and much
  more.

Guyana is currently divided into ten administrative Regions.
Each is run by an elected Regional Democratic Council. Each
of these are in turn divided into Neighbourhood Democratic
Councils which are responsible for solving problems and
initiating development projects in the areas for which they have
responsibility.. There are 65 of these Councils which have a
number of villages within their jurisdiction. As the foregoing
extracts from the interviews suggest, this attempt at Local
Government reorganisation pleased no one. Not even the
reorganisers themselves, as the next few paragraphs demonstrate.
There is now a cross party task force on Local Government
reform.

In contrast to what the people want it is instructive to look
at the ambivalence in what a leading political party offers in
the name of Local Government Reform. It is taken from the
PNC's submission to the Constitutional Reform Commission
(1999) and is similar in its arguments to those of the other
main political parties. One should remember, of course, that
it was the PNC which initiated the 1980 Local Government
changes. It reads:

> Local Government is the hub around which our democratic system
> should revolve. There can be no democracy without a strong,
> vibrant local government system. This system would provide for
> the decentralisation of power, the devolution of authority, and
> the participation of large numbers of people in the decision-making,
> management and development process in their communities. Local
> Government ought to provide the most obvious example of
> inclusionary democracy in action.[27]

As a set of general aims for local government the foregoing statement is impeccable. Implemented at independence, Guyana might have been well on its way to acquiring the inter-communal understanding, trust, and commitment so necessary for the making of the Guyanese. But instead of focusing on community development the submission goes on to argue for more of the same – large regional councils which the people regard as amorphous, anonymous and alienating. They do nothing for the physical, social, or spiritual growth of their communities. They satisfy none of the declared aims. It is still top down.

The submission goes on to argue for the full implementation of the Party's 1980 State Paper entitled 'A Reorganisation of Local Government'. In this, at least, there is the recognition that local government institutions should not be merely agencies of central government:

> Unfortunately, the proposals in that State Paper were never implemented as recommended.
> We believe that a bold effort should now be made to implement them with some adjustments. There should be clear understanding and acceptance that the Regional Democratic Councils and the smaller Local Democratic Organs are part of the Local Government system and not agencies of the Central Government. To this end, therefore, the Regional Democratic Councils should now be organised accordingly. They should exercise the power to raise revenues by taxation and otherwise and be responsible for a range of activities in their respective Regions as identified by law...

It is important to labour the following points because they are important in themselves and central to the arguments of the book.

- If Guyana is to become a truly functioning democracy the movement from colonial subjecthood to engaged citizenry is vital.
- Village community development must provide that starting point and growth to aid in the evolution of a Guyanese people.
- Given the size of the village communities, there is real

opportunity for all who so desire to discuss and decide upon matters pertinent to their welfare. This would provide a rare, true access to genuine participatory democracy.

- Cooperating to satisfy real welfare needs provides practical opportunities to acquire habits of democratic thought and action. Such a milieu of shared interests and rational problem solving encourages the growth of an ethos of teamwork. Successful outcomes to joint projects breed respect and confidence, however grudging at first, and in time provide foundational values for peaceful coexistence in a plural society.
- To continue to organise local government in large, bureaucratic, top-down administrative units would be to miss the opportunity, once again, to work outward from community building to nation building
- The latter above all, must be the test of all political action in this period of transition.
- To deny the Guyanese working class this opportunity for growth on the spurious grounds that the people are not yet ready would be to keep them forever subjects of their political parties and electoral fodder for the Guyanese political elite. Readiness can only come out of opportunities to be ready.
- The last point put differently is this. Does the Guyanese political elite have any vision of what it might do to build a nation or a state in which all its members are provided with equal opportunities to become active and involved citizens?

This focus is anything but new. On March 4, 1966, two months before independence, *New World,* the radical fortnightly journal of Guiana, carried a feature article from an American Community Development worker entitled 'Community Development – Key To National Regeneration'. In it he set out "to show the central role in nation building that community development can play, in both the economic and political spheres."[28] The writer, R. Brown, continues:

...it begins with the community as a unit and with the people's overall needs as they define them, rather than with a body of technical information which is thought by technicians, politicians or bureaucrats to be good for them... By this approach the knowledge of technicians is used only to the extent that it is required to solve technical problems first acknowledged by the community itself.

The ultimate measure of success is not statistics of miles of canals dug, acres newly under cultivation, livestock vaccinated, etc. important as these tangible results are. Rather, the focus is on what happens to people, the rationalisation of their attitudes, their growth in self-confidence, and their ability to solve problems peaceably, establish collective priorities, and work together for the common good... The goal of community development is to help people prepare themselves with the skills, attitudes, and institutions appropriate to their full participation in an economically independent and politically democratic nation-state.

The writer goes on to examine the economic aspects of social action. He discusses the modernisation approach to development and concludes that these arguments "are sophisticated but specious justifications for continuing the tradition of dependency on outsiders and postponing the day when local people will have to get down to the business of building their own nation with their own sweat... By applying under-utilised labour, land materials, capital and most of all enthusiasm and imagination, rural and urban communities could make an enormous contribution to their own well-being and prosperity." With the emphasis on fuller utilisation of indigenous resources he then goes on to discuss the important variables in turn. These are: savings and investment, entrepreneurial skills, markets, foreign exchange, desire for economic improvement, technical skills, and government organisation and administration.

On political action Brown is concerned about the relationship between community development and "the growth of national unity through expanded participation in democratic processes of problem-solving and cooperative action. One basic prerequisite of political responsibility is that individual men and women have confidence in the power to improve their lot." Colonial control, he argues, denied involvement and produced dependency. Community development, in contrast, provides the opportunities for involvement in decision-making, for making rational choices, and assuming responsibility for the consequences of those choices. Responsibility, in turn, breeds confidence in one's abilities and nurtures thoughtful political judgement. He goes on:

> What better way to gain such confidence than by starting with small successes, little projects that are responsive to the felt needs of the people who carry them out, projects which are theirs and from which they can gain a pride of accomplishment. Economic success is most persuasive. People gain confidence when they see that they have created new industries, better farming methods, improved marketing services as well as better health and educational facilities. The wider the community participation and the greater the community investment, the more likely is this social and psychological effect to be achieved.

Guyana has its share of successful community development projects. The work of The Beacon Foundation, a Guyanese NGO, especially among the Amerindians, is an outstanding 21st century example of how people-led projects can be successfully conducted. There are also government supported individual, cooperative and community projects. The argument here is to permeate the entire country with the village as the responsible generating focus.

It bears emphasis that what I am arguing for is a transfer of power and authority which is function led, not the consequence of a grand design which comes out of a fertile intellectual imagination. Such a transfer of real power and authority will, however, require a change of public philosophy, institutions and behaviour. As part of the development of that public philosophy for Guyana the rest of this chapter will examine the theoretical and practical claims of Functionalism as democracy at work and therefore a working peace and development system.

4. The Idea of Functional Cooperation Revisited.

The argument here is that competitive party politics in the manner of the Anglo-American model has failed to produce a working democracy for Guyana. The main reason for this is that the model has a minimum requirement of homogeneity for success. Guyana has been unable to produce any semblance of this requirement because its politics is dominated by ethnic cleavages and division. The result is that while the former is able to deal with its internal conflicts through open discussion, choice and the rule of law, in Guyana it is non-cooperation, violence and its threat which dominate political behaviour. In such circumstances, since the declared intention is to maintain a unitary state, the challenge is to produce a consensus model of politics, one which by its very structure and operations could promote the development of open debate, choice, the rule of law, and the Cooperative Republic.

Functionalism, (used here as Functional Cooperation to distinguish it from its other usages, especially Structural Functionalism in sociology and Functionalism in biology) is one continental European contribution to that consensus model. The other is Power Sharing which will be discussed in the next chapter. Together, functional cooperation and power sharing set out to satisfy the existential needs of all the people. These needs, I have argued elsewhere,[29] are those for security, participation, identity, recognition, and distributive justice. It is the operational dynamic of these elements which is most likely to produce that unity in diversity, that community, which will make democracy work. From the vista of 2005 this is a monumental task. It cries out to be started now.

David Mitrany remains the guru of Functionalism in international relations. His main concern was making peace in a troubled world. In 1943 he published his major work *A Working Peace System*.[30] In this he argued "that the development of international economic and social cooperation is a major prerequisite for the ultimate solution of political conflicts and the elimination of war."[31] Functionalism is not without its critics but it remains an integral part of the debate about the direction in which its outstanding success – Europe – should go. I will return to this. For now, I am adapting the arguments to support my proposition that a peaceful Guyanese society is more likely to develop through identifying and solving local problems together in community centre, "workshop and marketplace"[32] than by fighting each other over unspecified and doubtful ends.

I take the view that if function-led institutions are good for the management of international relations then they must also be relevant to the growth of cooperative action in domestic relationships.

The assumptions of functionalism run like this:

Political conflict is not a function of innate human aggressiveness nor is it the consequence of original sin. It results from the prolonged defects in peoples' social and economic circumstances. "Poverty, misery, ill health, illiteracy, economic insecurity, social injustice, exploitation, discrimination – these are the factors which create the desperation, apathy, frustration, fear, cupidity and hatred", which[33] encourage the spread of violent conflict.

If this is true, and it has certainly become part of the conventional wisdom about the causes of conflict during the twentieth and twenty-first centuries, then the practical village approach, outlined earlier, to satisfy welfare needs, provides people with the possibility of a common focus. Poverty, disease, and poor education are deprivations around which a divided people might unite and fight. They are the difficult battles and if we are to win we will need to develop habits of collaboration and joint problem solving which cut across the vertical dividing lines of our society. These habits are in their turn essential for the growth of those minimum values which are necessary for an engaged citizenry and a working democracy. They are the real ends of our struggle.

This is also a plausible interpretation of what Professor Arthur Lewis means when he says that good institutions for postcolonial plural societies have to be thought "through from the foundations up."[34] Borrowing European class-based institutions which have taken centuries to develop with their practice of winner takes all, "is destructive of any prospects of building a nation in which different peoples might live together in harmony."[35]

Functionalism, as a means of resolving conflict probably takes an optimistic view of human rationality. The alternative is too distressing to contemplate. But there is hard evidence to support optimism. It has been called variously the Common Market, the European Economic Community, and today the European

Union. Until about six decades or so ago the nations of Europe killed each other by the millions at regular intervals. Today, they are so enmeshed in functional, cooperative undertakings that war between them is inconceivable. This is not to suggest that there is no disagreement, lively debate and often times anger but that they have evolved peaceful, though sometimes painstaking means – through consensus and compromise – of dealing with them.

The furious debate taking place today is about the institutional architecture of an expanding Europe. From six to a current twenty-seven and from the humble beginnings of the European Coal and Steel Community and the Atomic Energy Commission to the European Union, the claim is now that functionalism has outlived its usefulness. The dictum of 'form following function', it is now claimed, has enmeshed Europe in a cobweb of relationships and institutions which are now unclear and confusing. The time has now come it is argued, for institutional order to be imposed on such an amorphous functional form. What is to be the political crown for economic and social success? A Federal or United Europe? Or what?

This debate about the ultimate shape of Europe does not concern us. However, the greatest threat to the European future – lack of popular support for European institutions – does. Clearly many European citizens regard the EU as too centralised, too undemocratic, too remote from local concerns. This reinforces the argument of this chapter about the need for local democratic participation and control. If Guyana was ever to reach the position where successful cooperative relationships produce passionate debate about our institutional future and democratic advance, we would have achieved our first goal on the way to the Cooperative Republic.

So it bears repeating that for now and in the foreseeable future what Guyana wants from local government is local cooperation across local boundaries to produce development in all its forms for all its people. Success here would bring with it those values of respect, confidence and trust and in turn make significant inroads into those more profound human needs for security, participation, recognition of identities and distributive justice.

These are the minimum requirements for the growth of the Guyanese and his/her embrace of a functioning democracy.

The next chapter will confront the problem of institutional change for central government. Cooperation is only likely to take root and grow on any significant scale at the local level, if it is mirrored in the thoughts and actions at the centre. It has already been argued that the existing competitive institutions in a divided society encourage political selfishness and greed. They stunt imaginative thought and creative political entrepreneurship. It follows therefore that only a political architecture which nurtures purposeful interaction is likely to produce that democratic movement which the country wishes. That institutional framework must be so constructed that power is shared equitably because only an enthusiastically sharing elite will be confident enough to recognise the importance, and so support the devolution of power and responsibility to the people.

END NOTES

1. Quoted in Knight, B, Chigudu, H and Tandon, M (2002)
   Reviving Democracy. Citizens at the Heart of Governance, pp. 83-
   84, Earthscan, London; and Sen, A. (1999), 'Democracy as a
   Universal Value', *Journal of Democracy,* 10.3, pp. 3-17, Johns
   Hopkins University Press, Washington, DC.
2. Mill, J.S. (1861), *Considerations on Representative Government,*
   p. 362, J.M. Dent & Son, (1910).
3. Rambushka, A. and Shepsle, K. (1972), *Politics in Plural
   Societies: A Theory of Democratic Instability,* p. 217, Merrill,
   Columbus, Ohio.
4. Kwayana, E. (1961), 'Common Sense About Power Sharing',
   www.guyanacaribbeanpolitics.com /commentary/powersharing
5. Lewis, A. (1965), *Politics in West Africa,* London, George Allen
   & Unwin.
6. Lijphart, A (1991), 'The Power Sharing Approach', in Montville,
   J. V. (1991), *Conflict and Peacemaking in Multiethnic Societies,* pp.
   491-509, Lexington Books, New York.
7. Mitrany, D, (1966), *A working Peace System,* p.36, Quadrangle
   Books, Chicago.
8. Taylor, C, (2001), ' Foreword', in Gagnon, A-G, and Tully, J.
   (2001), (eds) *Multinational Democracies,* CUP, Cambridge.
9. Quoted in Ramphal, S. (2003), 'Global Governance or New
   Imperium, Which is it going to be?' *Round Table,* Issue 369
   April 2003, Oxford, Carfax Publishing.
10. Taylor, P. (1968), 'The Concept of Community and the European
    Integration Process' in Hodges, M. (1972) *European Integration,*
    Harmondsworth, Penguin, pp. 205-210.
11. Barber, B.S. (1984), *Strong Democracy: Participatory Politics for
    a New Age*, London, University of California Press, p. xiv.
12. For a more detailed historical account of village administration
    from emancipation to independence see, Seecoomar, J. (2002),
    Contributions Towards the Resolution of Conflict in Guyana,, Leeds,
    Peepal Tree Press, pp.73-79.
13. See for instance Tota C. Mangar, 'Local Government experiment
    in Colonial British Guiana, *Stabroek News,* 8 August, 2002.
14. See *British Guiana: Memorandum of the Honourable A.M. Ashmore
    on the subject of Village Administration from the Time of the Abilition
    of Slavery to the present day, with an economic census of the villages
    of British Guiana for 1902*, Georgetown, Demerara, 1903.

15. *Report of the British Guiana Constitutional Commission* (The Robertson Report) CMD 9274, 1954, para 44.
16. Ibid., para 45
17. See R.T. Smith, 'Race, Class, Politics and Family Life: Hopetown in 1951-52' (http://home.uchicago.edu/~rts1/hopetown.htm), 2002.
18. 'The Hopetown Discussion Group', Ibid.
19. Leeds, Peepal Tree Press, 1987.
20. *The Last English Plantation*, pp. 169-170.
21. See Clem Seecharan, *Sweetening Bitter Sugar: Jock Campbell, the Booker Reformer in British Guiana 1934-1966*, Ian Randle Publishers, 2005, pp. 401-418, for an account of the programme to move the housing of estate workers off the sugar estates into private housing units.
22. See Odeen Ishmael, 'The Fraudulent Local Government Elections in 1979', *Guyana Journal*, Sept. 2007. Online at http://www.guyanajournal.com/local_govt_elections.html
23. In the December 1986 municipal elections, the PNC won all ninety-one seats in local government. On the basis of massive fraud in the 1985 general elections, when the PNC awarded itself 79% of the vote, the opposition boycotted the regional elections. See US Library of Congress, Country Studies, online at http://countrystudies.us/guyana/18.htm.
24. *See Stabroek News*, Leader, 'City Election Would Be A Farce', January 19, 2009. And see Europa World Year Book, 2004, p. 1979.
25. Ibid.
26. 'PNC Submission to the Constitutional Reform Commission', *New Nation,* Vol. 42, Issue 36, May 16-22, 1999.
27. Brown, R. (1966), 'Community Development – Key To National Regeneration.' in *New World,* Vol.1 No 35, 4.3.66, Georgetown, Guyana, pp. 13-21. The other quotations in this section are taken from this article.
28. Seecoomar, J. (2002), *Contributions Towards the Resolution Of Conflict in Guyana,* Leeds, Peepal Tree Press, Chap. 6.
29. Mitrany, D. (1943), *A Working Peace System,* London, Royal Institute of International Affairs
30. Ibid.
31. Claude, I. L. (1964) *Swords Into Ploughshares,* New York, Random House, p. 345.
32. Mitrany, D. (1966) Introduction to Quadrangle Books edition, p. 25.

33. *Swords Into Ploughshares,* p. 347.
34. Lewis, W.A. (1965), *Politics in West Africa,* p. 64.
35. Ibid., p. 66.

CHAPTER THREE.

PARTICIPATORY DEMOCRACY:
CENTRAL GOVERNMENT

The grand design of this discourse is the development of a working democracy for a deeply divided multiracial Guyana. The argument so far has been that a precondition for this design is the growth of a 'people', that is Guyanese who have become citizens because they have shaken off the debilitating effects of subjecthood, obedience, and the myopic constraints of race; a citizenry that has emerged through active engagement with things that really matter, in other words, responsibility for important aspects of their own welfare. The tests of all this being achieved would be the gradual growth of good faith, the return of trust and an ever increasing commitment to the Guyanese general good.

Some would contend that putting local before central government is a cart before the horse argument; that before power and responsibility can be devolved ungrudgingly, there must be government at the centre which is philosophically convinced that the liberation of the people is an important goal and that the devolution of power is one important means by which to achieve it. This is probably true, but as every Guyanese carpenter worth his salt knows, the superstructure will blow over in the wind unless the foundations are firm. Arthur Lewis's dictum that in societies like ours, "good political institutions have to be thought through from the foundations up" lends intellectual support to common sense. A case will therefore be made in this chapter for government which is constructed to share legislative and executive power among all the elected representatives of the people. The intimate interplay between the centre and its roots, after all, must come nearest to the true meaning of democracy as government of, by, and for the people.

In fact part of the current political debate in Guyana concentrates on just this. So before I make my own contribution, it is important to review the existing ideas of Guyanese, Caribbean and other international thinkers on this vitally important debate about the nature of democracy, democratic institutions and democratic governance, especially for polarised plural societies.

(1). Power Sharing: The David Hinds' View.

In my view we can do no better than start with David Hind's thoughtful and wide-ranging challenge. That is, his Walter Rodney Memorial Lecture, 'Race, Democracy, and Power Sharing' (19. 07. 03.)[1]

David Hinds bases his argument for the need for Power-Sharing on the failure of Guyanese to make liberal democratic institutions work, and the politics to which this has given rise since independence. Its outcomes have been "racial insecurity and competition, undemocratic rule and the attendant political and economic instability."[2] Putting it more starkly Dr. Hinds says, "Governance in Guyana has, therefore, evolved into an exercise in political witch-hunting, party domination, marginalisation of the losing faction, plunder of state resources as a means of personal enrichment and maintenance of state clientelism. And opposition has meant the destabilisation of the government."[3] Such a politics threatens social disintegration, authoritarian government and economic stagnation. Faced with these ruinous possibilities Hinds argues for "the need to transform the formal democracy that currently exists into a substantive democracy based on peoples power, political and racial equality, equality of opportunity both socially and racially, and shared nationhood."[4] Paraphrasing Kwayana's 1961 proposal he asserts that power sharing fits the democratic need because it "springs from the very concrete situation in the country."[5]

Dr. Hinds usefully traces the history of the idea of Power-Sharing for Guyana.[6] Eusi Kwayana takes pride of place as the originator. He recognised and articulated publicly in 1961 that neither of the two major race groups, for a number of historical reasons, was going to accept the other as leader.[7] Winning and losing therefore had to be eradicated from the Guyanese political lexicon and sharing, in one form or another, had to take their places. Note is also taken of the fact that Professor Arthur Lewis in his 1965 Whidden Lectures on *Politics in West Africa* made a powerful case for power sharing as the democratic approach to governance in the plural postcolonial societies of West Africa. Tellingly, he argued that "the democratic problem in a plural society is to create institutions which give all the various groups the opportunity to participate in decision making, since only then can they feel that they are full members of a nation, respected by their numerous brethren and giving equal respect to the natural bond which holds them together."[8] Both men, Kwayana (1961) and Lewis, (1965) wrote before the latter-day guru of power sharing, Arend Lijphart, made his entrance (1968).[9] The latter has become the acknowledged international scholar on the problems of governance in ethnically divided societies and both Hinds and the PNCR have made full use of this in their proposals.

Two assumptions are fundamental to Lijphart's work. The first is that "stable democracy is possible in deeply divided societies," if the elites of opposing groups "are willing and able to systematically counteract the tendencies towards conflict."[10] The second is that, partition and secession apart, power sharing is the only political form through which this stability can be made to happen. In his own words Lijphart says, "I still believe that consociational democracy (power sharing) is not only the optimal form of democracy for deeply divided societies but also for the most deeply divided countries, the only feasible form."[11]

There are four important elements for which constitutional designers must provide, if power sharing is to achieve its objectives. These are:

(a)   Executive Power-Sharing. That is, a grand coalition of representatives from all significant groups in the government of the country.

(b)   Group Autonomy. This means joint decisions in matters of general concern but the freedom of separate groups to organise and run their own internal affairs.

(c)   Proportionality. This is the standard for the allocation of political representation, resources and public appointments.

(d)   The minority veto. This is the ultimate protection through which the vital interests of minorities are protected.[12]

Lijphart is not without his severe critics, especially in the applicability of his model to postcolonial, multi-ethnic, societies. They point out that his examples of success are mainly Western European – Belgium, the Netherlands and Switzerland – among others. Those which failed over time include Cyprus, Lebanon and Colombia. One explanation offered for this variation is the longer Western European historical tradition of elite accommodation in matters of conflict management, while in most postcolonial societies the dominant approach to political problems is elite conflict rather than cooperation. It must be pointed out, however, that pre-colonial societies had highly developed systems of negotiation and compromise for dispute resolution at the tribal and village levels, and modern constitutional designers might do well to look again at their prior historical and cultural inheritances in the search for institutions which are authentically theirs.

Critics therefore emphasise that the heavy dependence on the need to shift from elite conflict to cooperation is fundamentally optimistic, and without this it makes the threat of failure at the start, very real. Vetoes can easily give rise to gridlock and in societies with ethnic majorities, proportionality can further institutionalise majoritarian instead of consensus politics. Moreover, to insist that executive power sharing is the only feasible approach to the problems of governance in deeply divided societies is to shut out thought on other forms which might be more in keeping with the historical and cultural demands of any given society.[13]

In Guyana the idea of power sharing continued to titillate throughout the rest of the twentieth century. Politicians sniffed and ran away and then sniffed suspiciously again. Winning and the smell of power, however, were far more stimulating for them. The start of the current century has seen the idea become resurgent and persistent. This review is based on those resurgent contributions.

Having demonstrated the mismatch between democratic institutions and undemocratic politics, Hinds goes on to make his case for a power-sharing democracy and congruence between institutions and behaviour. He assumes that the Guyanese wish to live together in "peaceful coexistence, cooperation and mutual respect."[14] He contends that whatever changes are agreed must be written into law and not left to chance. The principle of proportionality in Executive allocations and the operational rules governing those allocations being the most important.

A focus for this grand coalition is a generally agreed programme for national development (see Appendix 5). High quality, bold, and imaginative leadership is pivotal if such revolutionary changes are to bring success. Hinds goes on to deal with the critiques of the idea and its practice. He examines some of the reasons for success and failure in some of the countries in which power sharing has been tried. He deals with the specific charges of gridlock in decision-making, the hardening of racial voting patterns, the absence of political opposition, elite domination and the rejection of Westminster-style democracy and counters them briefly, logically and with reason. Before he gives his own institutional proposals for a power-sharing government in Guyana, he ends his discourse thus: "Elite control of power is a given in Guyana. But a 'vertical power sharing' or devolution of power to the local governments can counterbalance this. In this regard, he sees the return to village government is key to power sharing. It allows for both racial and class empowerment – racial because of the relative ethnic homogeneity of our villages, and class because more working-class people are likely to be elected to village councils."[15]

Before dealing with the nature of the institutional changes suggested by Hinds, note must be taken of his analytical technique. In the metaphor of the journey, he assesses why and how we have got to where we are today. He then examines what our destination might be and how we might get there and provides benchmarks to keep us on our assigned tracks. This analytical model is used in the rest of the work to examine the other contributions to the power-sharing debate. The lecture is therefore included as Appendix Two at the end of this book.

In order to achieve his aim of a fair, functioning and inclusive democratic society, Hinds suggests three inviolable criteria for institutional reconstruction. These are: proportional representation, separation of powers and checks and balances. In his necessarily brief outline, the functions and responsibilities of the executive, legislative, and civil society branches of government are summarized

It is proposed that the executive should comprise a proportionally elected two or three person executive presidency, (that is, a president, a prime minister, a deputy prime minister) and a cabinet. In addition to their individual responsibilities, the three person inner cabinet would have considerable joint powers. They would be able to approve or veto bills passed by parliament, nominate the top officials for the rule of law and the civil service, and hire and fire members of the cabinet, among others.

The legislature would be bi-cameral with an elected People's House of Representatives (PHR) and a nominated Chamber of Civil Society (CSS). He outlines the functions of each chamber, with the PHR, for instance, having 'no confidence' voting rights over the executive, powers of dispute settlement and the passing of bills. Presumably this also means being able to reject bills proposed by the executive presidency. The CCS, nominated from the great and the good in Guyana, would have review and delaying powers over proposed legislation.

Finally, local government would be restored to the villages with the regional councils having oversight and supervisory powers.

David Hinds' thoughts and ideas are in the public domain

and are part of the questioning, discussion and choice which the Guyanese people as a whole must eventually make. This debate cannot be conducted in these pages but a few important issues cannot be ignored. The first concerns the practical workings of the executive presidency and I can do no better than repeat the question put to me by an interviewee in 1998. He said, "Yuh eva hear bout two man driving a dankey cart or a moto car? The bloody ting doan work. He/she will need to be educated about the possibilities." This is the same criticism of the optimistic assumption made about elite cooperation when their recent history has been of implacable dissent on political change. The second concerns the number of points of veto. In a country guided more by suspicion than by trust, it requires a tremendous leap of the imagination not to believe that multiple vetoes would produce more deadlock than movement. This would increase uncertainty and postpone that growth of confidence, citizenship, and democracy even further. The fate of local government elections since 1994 is an obvious example of the kind of log-jam that could so easily occur.

The final point concerns the linchpin of the power-sharing discourse – the principle of proportionality. In a society like Guyana with one ethnic group having a clear majority, proportionality does not guarantee equity. This then raises the spectre of the return of winning and losing, together with its attendant ills, even before they have been laid to rest. Although Hinds downplays the 7% difference,[17] it has to be pointed out that the PPP/C have been winning elections on this majority since 1992. Indeed, in the elections of 2006, the proportion of the vote obtained by PNCR declined sharply.[18] Remember 1964? PR was to be the panacea. PR also denies the widely expressed wish of many Guyanese for directly electing their representatives, and of course, the system of party slates concentrates power in the hands of the party elite. This is a very real problem and it cries out for solution.

(2). Power Sharing: The Peoples' National Congress Reform (PNCR) View.

Despite positive rumblings in the ranks for sometime before the party officially shifted its position, the PNCR became firm participants in the Power Sharing discourse during the second half of 2002. This was after the late Leader, Desmond Hoyte, who had argued throughout most of his political life that strong opposition was essential to effective government, had given his blessing to the idea of "adjusted governance". The official Party document *Shared Governance*[19] was published in Guyana on October 16, 2002 and posted on the Guyana Caribbean Politics website on 6 Dec. 2002.

The document begins with twelve 'Principles Underpinning Shared Governance'[20] and three conditions which the Party deemed to be favourable to "multiparty governance in Guyana."[21] It then went on to deal with its suggestions for institutional change and their operations.[22]

The overarching aim of the new system would be to satisfy the developmental aspirations of all Guyanese. The principles of proportionality and inclusion should be the guide for the allocation of executive responsibility, decision-making, and resource distribution. Institutional arrangements must be enshrined to promote consensus, resolve disputes, advance fairness and keep the functioning of such fundamental changes under continuous review. The focus of all this is to be a generally agreed programme for national development.

These are fundamental guides for a deeply divided society in search of reconstruction, but there is a puzzling principle. It reads. "The larger the margin of victory of the winning party, the fewer should be the inhibitions to the exercise of its powers in the multi-party executive."[23] Does this mean that 'sharing' is to be a temporary expedient and that 'winning' is to remain the desired end state? The majoritarian view is also hostage to a situation in which one of the two main parties fractures or loses support – without that electoral support seeing itself as in any sense represented by the party in power. The dangers of having sections of the Guyanese population – say the

Georgetown-based Afro-Guyanese working class – feeling totally disenfranchised and unrepresented, even in the parliamentary opposition, must be regarded as an alarming prospect. Power sharing if it means anything, must mean the development of a new political culture which has cooperation, consensus and justice for all at its centre. It is a fragile concept precisely because it seeks to remove the power trappings of winning, losing and, literally, muscular opposition. Any halfhearted entry to the principle of power sharing, with the other eye on the main chance, could only mean more suffering and failure. It is the fundamental weakness of the principle of proportionality, in a racially polarised society. This principle needs considerably more thought and clarification.

The Party (PNCR) sees the ability to discuss constitutional reforms jointly, ideological convergence, international support for progress and increased 'partiocracy', i.e., the increased effectiveness of the parties in controlling their supporters, as favourable conditions for shared governance. 'Partiocracy' is the puzzling concept here. It is no secret that the entrepreneurial use of racial anxieties over the last fifty years by the Guyanese political elite has not only produced strongly polarised party loyalty, it has contributed substantially to the existing evils in the society. One would therefore assume that when a serious attempt is being made to move the country away from the politics of an unending struggle for control in order to protect against domination, to a politics based on sharing for the benefit of all, that a new meaning of 'partiocracy' would be spelt out. This ought to be one which sets out not only to enhance the participation of the party rank and file, but also to gradually and deliberately to loosen the bonds of race, and promote the growth of relationships and loyalties based on reason and choice. One can argue that it is not least the centralisation of power within the parties by their respective elites that has contributed to the lack of influence or control experienced by ordinary citizens. From this standpoint it is to be regretted that the PNCR's document does not attempt a rationale for such fundamental change and its expected outcomes. The people must be trusted with the arguments about why changes are being made in their name if their reasoned support is to be guaranteed. The people's understanding that the new institutions have ethical foundations would be a vital element in their transition, at last, from bondsmen/women to citizen. In its turn, the fusion of institutions with a public acceptance of their underlying philosophy would mean a political architecture able to withstand any opportunistic attempts at overthrow.

As a starting point for institutional design, the PNCR document of October 16, 2002, indicates boundaries within which the discussions, negotiations and agreements for shared governance might take place. The centrepiece would be a mutually agreed Coalition Agreement.[24] This would include as its remit, policy programmes taken from the national development plan, portfolio allocations (the PNCR flags up its own proposals in Section VI: 'Allocation of Ministerial Portfolios') and the process of making decisions. The latter, the document argues, should have transparency, consensus and responsibility as its working goals.

By way of institutions the document suggests:[25]

- A non-executive Head of State, appointed for a seven year, renewable term. Apart from the decorative trappings, he/she will have certain specific functions concerning assent and dispute resolution. The document recognises that the protocols for dispute resolution will need to be negotiated.
- A Council of Ministers (Cabinet) with near universal powers of decision and implementation. This includes all policy issues, financial commitments, new legislation, and public appointments, among the other important concerns of government.
- A Standing Coalition Management Committee. A committee of leaders, that, as the name implies, manages the coalition and is the highest forum for dispute resolution.
- In the new era, the role of Parliament would be different but not diminished. It would retain powers of lawmaking, financial control and scrutiny. Public debates

and select committee inquisition would provide "for citizens, interest groups, independent MPs, non-government parties and other stakeholders to influence the actions of government."[26] The party is concerned to avoid a new era of executive dictatorship and so proposes additional safeguards which would open up the decision-making process to the participation and scrutiny of the public and civic society.

By way of working practices the document suggests:

- Ministerial Working Groups. These are sub-committees of the all powerful Council of Ministers wherein the real complexities involved in making decisions are examined in order to present the Cabinet with options for choice and action.
- Procedures for Unresolved Issues. These are classified according to whether they are deemed harmful to race relations or deemed matters of "party distinction". The process is more elaborate in concerns of race. A dispute that began in the Cabinet, could then go to Parliament, and finally to the Head of State who, in conjunction with the Ethnic Relations Commission, must decide whether or not the matter is harmful. Deemed inimical, the matter must be withdrawn or amended for resubmission to the Cabinet. "If the Head of State rules that the matter is not harmful to race relations, the matter could be implemented and is considered a collective decision of the Council".

The PNCR makes it clear that this is a discussion document and that if anything is to come of it there will be need for clarification, discussion, and debate before adjustments and choices are made. This important document about a matter of profound seriousness in the life of Guyana comes from a major political party. It is therefore included as Appendix Three to this book.

(3) Power Sharing: The Peoples Progressive Party/ Civic (PPP/C) View.

The foregoing proposals of Dr. Hinds and those of the PNCR are two examples of power sharing by grand coalition. That is, on the principle of proportionality, parties agree to share executive power under an elaborate system of scrutiny and controls by Parliament and the people.

In contrast, the PPP/C argues "for power sharing at the level of the legislature."[27] As the elected government since 1992, the PPP/C does not believe that executive power sharing would make significant inroads into the problems of governance in Guyana. They contend that without the preconditions of good faith and trust, power sharing at the executive level would lead inevitably to gridlock and this could be worse than the current problems of governance. Instead they claim, that, since 1992, there has been intermittent dialogue to make existing Guyanese political institutions more inclusive. The result of this ten-year effort, they claim, has been an impressive set of agreed reforms, some of which are already written into law while others are waiting to find themselves into the statute books. Fully implemented and working, the Party claims "these and other reforms make the Guyana Constitution the most advanced in terms of inclusiveness and opposition involvement in governance in the Caribbean region and certainly one of the most advanced in the world."[28] They therefore argue that the time has come to make these hard-fought-for changes work and not to look for more radical changes. They argue that the combination of existing reforms and the radical power-sharing changes proposed would inflict a rate and burden of change which would be impossible to handle and likely to be self-destructive. They are convinced that the gradualism of the proposed Legislative changes would promote cooperation and help to rekindle trust. In time the conditions might be right for the successful adaptation of other forms of power sharing.

In its paper "Building Trust to Achieve Genuine Political Co-operation,"[29] the PPP/C government offers a historical sweep of its involvement "in the political campaign for good governance."[30] It points out that since the unified anti-colonial movement foundered in 1955, the PPP has "made continuous efforts to arrive at arrangements with the PNC to maintain and ensure the unity of the Guyanese people. These efforts were particularly intense during the periods 1961 to 1964, 1976 to 1978 and 1984 to 1985. The PNC rejected these efforts categorically describing them at one time as 'superficially attractive'."[31]

In 1992 a PPP/C government took office and began the process of constitutional reform with the commitment to make the governing of Guyana more inclusive and participatory. By 1997 a Select Committee had collected volumes of evidence from across the country but further progress was suspended because of the demands of the 1997 General Elections.

The PPP/C won again and a period of sustained destabilisation began. CARICOM, the regional organisation was invited to intervene, and the PPP/C agreed to a reduced term in office and more substantial achievements in the constitutional reform process. The result has been an impressive list of agreements and constitutional amendments but little implementation, not least because the necessary acts of cooperation, for whatever reason, have not been forthcoming.[32] The reform process continued after the 2001 elections and in the PPP/C's view putting the agreements on

- Establishing five Standing Committees to examine and review government policy in the social, economic, foreign policy and natural resources sectors;
- A Parliamentary Management Committee;
- An Ethnic Relations Commission;
- A Standing Committee on Constitutional Reform; among many others,

to work, would not only make for inclusiveness, it would rekindle trust and make greater and more beneficial change possible. In a word, the PPP/C believes that a working, inclusive Parliamentary system can provide more effective and sharing government than a formidably complex executive power-sharing organisation can do. It must be borne in mind that until the second half of 2002, the other major Guyanese political party held a similar view. Consequently, all the changes were negotiated within the boundaries of making Parliament more inclusive and effective.

The PPP/C is probably right when it claims that, fully implemented, the amendments to the constitution would make parliamentary government in Guyana inclusive and advanced. In my view, however, all improvements would be inadequate until the problem 'of periodic changes of government' is met head-on and resolved satisfactorily. To Guyanese outside the core of the PPP/C's ethnic support, its position is unlikely to be seen as other than an unwillingness to make more than token moves towards inclusiveness: inclusion, maybe, but on our majoritarian terms. In fairness, one must see the PPP/C's stance in the context of a period when the PNCR appeared to be attempting to advance its argument for power sharing by a cynical strategy of proxy violence designed to make Guyana ungovernable. Few fairly elected governments would have seen much virtue in conceding the power-sharing argument in such circumstances. And yet, for one party to win, and go on winning, by whatever means, and so shut out the other from access to real power, is to continue to provide the conditions for disaffection, disillusion and conflict. The rest of this chapter attempts another confrontation with this dilemma.

The PPP/C government paper, 'Building Trust To Achieve Genuine Political Cooperation' is included as Appendix Four.

Most of the other Guyanese and Caribbean academic and political commentators have opted to support the idea of the grand coalition for Guyana. In these circumstances, it is worth pointing out that Lijphart himself is doubtful about the workability of this model for ethnically divided societies where one of the major cleavages has a clear majority. In fact he states categorically that "one of the two most serious unfavourable factors for power sharing is the presence of a majority ethnic group."[34] The second is the presence "of large socio-economic differences among the ethnic groups."[35] But Lijphart is not to be deterred. Driven by his belief that peacemaking in multi-ethnic societies is best served by power sharing, he lets his imagination roam freely, but his method to overcome the disadvantage of a majority ethnic group comes with a health warning. "Considerable caution should be exercised before the method is adopted."[36] He writes:

> It consists of majority under-representation and minority over-representation or, in its more far-reaching form, parity of representation for all ethnic groups. For instance a group comprising 80% of the population might be given only 70% or 60% of the seats in Parliament and the ministerial positions in the cabinet or even, in the case of parity, only 50%; and the representation of the minority or minorities would be increased correspondingly.[37]

How far does Lijphart's reservations about the power sharing model in circumstances of there being an ethnic group with a clear majority and with major socio-economic differences between groups apply to Guyana? We have already noted that the actual majority/minority differences are not huge, but this could be distorted by the fact that there may be different levels of electoral loyalty to the two main parties amongst the ethnic groups that generally support them. On the evidence of elections between 1992 and 2006 this would, indeed, seem to be the case. On the issue of socio-economic difference, the reality is complex. The reality is that poverty relates most strongly to geographical location and occupation. Unquestionably, extreme poverty in located in the interior, and the poverty of Afro and Indo-Guyanese is relative in comparison to poverty amongst Guyana's Amerindians. Outside the interior, poverty is concentrated amongst self-employed agricultural labourers and non-agricultural labourers in the rural areas; in the urban areas, casual (and frequently unemployed) labourers are the group most affected by poverty. However, in Guyana, given the historical distribution of occupations along ethnic lines, the connections between poverty and ethnicity are inescapable. There are significant differences between the poverty levels amongst Afro-Guyanese (27.5%) and Indo-Guyanese (12%) – though both pale against the 56% of Amerindians living in poverty – and in the vexed political context of Guyana these differences can become another source of perceived discrimination.[38] Since these figures relate to 1992-93, after 28 years of Afro-Guyanese political domination, the issues of poverty and economic marginalisation would seem to be more properly regarded as the outcome of elite rather than ethnic domination. However, whilst properly empirical studies concerning the facts of actual voting behaviour and the actual distribution of poverty and wealth may be lacking in Guyana, the perception of Indian wealth and African poverty held by many Afro-Guyanese add a further element of toxicity to relations.

So with respect to Lijphart's reservations, in Guyana, where bad blood and mistrust between the party elites seem to grow rather than diminish, this manipulated version of the grand coalition seems to be a non-starter. For grand coalition politics is elite-driven and political stability therefore depends on their ability to break out of ethnic confines in order to compromise and accommodate. Such a sharp break from conflict to cooperation is optimism personified.

This does not mean that power sharing cannot be made to work in ex-colonial multi-ethnic societies. What it does mean is that institutions for these societies, following Professor Arthur Lewis, have to be carefully crafted from the foundations upward and this is crucial whether we borrow and /or invent new designs. In other words power sharing for Guyana has to be designed by Guyanese to meet the specific needs of all Guyanese. They have to be special because the Guyanese demographic configuration is special.

Power-Sharing: An Alternative To The Grand Coalition.

It seems to me that the main stumbling block to the proper functioning of Parliamentary democracy in Guyana is the critically important proviso that the opposition should be a government in waiting. That is, that there should be periodic changes of government through keenly contested elections based on programmatic offerings. From the late 1950s onwards, it became clear that as long as race continued to be the electoral driving force only one side would go on winning; that electoral democracy does not produce equal access to the state and its distributions. To those who, at different times, were threatened with permanent loss, the electoral process soon became irrelevant and the consignment to eternal opposition an insult and a grotesque misrepresentation of parliamentary democracy. The consequence has been a mismatch between the demands of democratic institutions and the practice of politics which has been persistently non-democratic.

This mismatch has manifested itself in the spiralling effects of adversarial politics, fraud, muscular street opposition, economic stagnation and widespread disenchantment, disillusion, and despair. To be fair, substantial sections of the people and the political intelligentsia have always recognised the explosive threats latent in this unfortunate, historically-given situation. From the 1960s onward, they have presented a steady stream of argument for power sharing in one or other of its many guises in order to promote cooperation and reduce conflict. Recently those clamours for a working democracy instead of a voting democracy[39] have become louder and more insistent. In a sea of uncertainty and doubt this is probably the most hopeful sign that the Cooperative Republic will survive and grow.

Most of the current discourse has centred on the model of the grand coalition with proportionality and mutual vetoes as the guiding principles. Parties share executive powers and responsibility and have as their focus the needs and aspirations of all the Guyanese people. These take tangible form in a generally agreed programme for national development. The entire operation is to be facilitated by a system of committees for increased participation including oversight, scrutiny and dispute resolution.[40]

At first glance, and if the relevant postcolonial evidence is to be believed, the proposed power-sharing system would be so hemmed in by controls and lack of good faith, it would be immobilised before it begins. Since Guyana has one ethnic group with a clear majority, the principle of proportionality quickly reintroduces the spectre of winning and losing and all its attendant ills. But I do not want to spend time criticising this Lijphartian discourse of the promised land.

What I want to do is to suggest a less complex alternative as part of the debate. It is called alternating government. Rotating government will also do. What I have in mind is this. The life of a parliament would be set at five years and each of the two main political parties would take charge of government for one term. The party in opposition then becomes in every sense, a government in waiting. Opposition becomes responsible but forever vigilant, and critical when necessary. The inevitable contact between cabinet and shadow cabinet, in the interest of good government for all, begins the journey to habits of collaboration and cooperation and removes the premium from wrecking as a political end. After all, both groups can say, 'We will be government next time round.' In time, say after one or two cycles, the people might be asked to vote on whether or not a government, based purely on its performance, should be allowed a second term. This would be the maximum consecutive period for which any single government might hold office. Above all, alternating government makes certain that each party is constitutionally guaranteed regular access to that human need for real control and the pride and dignity which comes with it. Control, according to Sites,[41] is "the basis of social order". The human needs specified at regular intervals throughout this and the previous work are sub-sets of the overarching need for control. Satisfy them and the need for control is also satisfied.

Parties in opposition do not only want a piece of the action to distribute the resources of the country in their own way. They genuinely believe they can be more efficient, less corrupt and more accountable to all. With demands for justice and fairness as their battle cry, they will not be satisfied with indefinite periods in the wilderness, however much opposition power they wield. At this stage, in the current Guyanese context, Lijphartian power sharing cannot be a substitute for real power and authority. In this latter sense, and it cannot be overstressed, "the sharing of power is a prerequisite for dignity as well as self – and mutual respect".[42]

The involvement of the people in elections and voting takes on heightened importance, but before I deal with this I want to pay some attention to the social and economic content of these five yearly cycles. In keeping with the thinking of the Guyanese political elite, this is to be based on a detailed national development plan. Even though it is ultimately the work of technicians, the people must be encouraged to contribute their thoughts and ideas about their poverty, health care, education, housing, employment and other concerns before the plan is put together. Detailed consultations and explanations must be provided at different points before final acceptance is asked for. After all, it is the peoples' welfare which is at stake and they need to know how that is to be provided for them along each step of the way. It is this understanding of how the quality of their lives is to be the focus of development which will encourage their support.

Apart from providing five-yearly criteria for accountability, the involvement of the people in the planning for national development is crucial to their emancipation from the subjecthood of the colonial and postcolonial periods and their own development as thoughtful and engaged citizens, the latter being the indispensable end of a functioning democracy. To deny them this right to participation on the spurious grounds of non-readiness is to collude with a denial of freedom for selfish ends.

At various points throughout this chapter, reference has been made to the intimate relationship between political change and economic development. More specifically, the economic arguments have been tied up with general support for a National Development Strategy from which governments are expected to develop their action programmes and which will act as tests for their accountability.

The Strategy which exists is the result of lengthy collaboration between national and international expertise together with some input from the people. It deals with macroeconomic strategy, social policy, the productive sectors and the infrastructure. Together these sections run to 5 volumes and can be read on the dedicated website: www.guyana.org/NDS/NDS.htm. Because of its centrality to progress, a summary of the NDS is included as Appendix 5 at the end of this book.

Appendices 3 to 5 are included for another important reason. It is that, given the intimate linkage between democracy, peace and development, these papers indicate a preparedness to make that leap from ideas, to serious collaboration, to action. Appendix 1 outlines one approach – facilitated problem solving – through which we might confront and resolve our political predicament. Appendix 2 – the paper by Hinds – provides an important view from outside the two main parties, but one that is particularly sensitive to the sense of Afro-Guyanese exclusion. This with the policy statements from PNCR, PPP/C and the NDS form an important part of the agenda. There is no difference between them that is insurmountable and the Guyanese can rightly claim an advanced state of readiness for peacemaking. Elite courage must make the leap.

With the question of who should govern decided by constitutional provision, the primary voting responsibilities of the people would be to choose their representatives and to decide on matters of fundamental constitutional change. 'Their representatives' means the return of the constituency MP. There has been a persistent clamour for this reversion to single member constituencies since it was removed by PR. The reasons are on the grounds of identification, accountability and intimacy. Constituency MPs provide that important feedback and monitoring conduit between central government and people. It is one vital aspect of real participation in action and provides a return of influence to rank and file parliamentary representatives against the overwhelming power of the party elites. In Art. 48 of 'Shared Governance' the PNCR makes additional provision for popular access to Parliament when it says:

> The practice of public petitions should be reactivated in Guyana politics. Citizens should be encouraged to submit petitions to parliament on matters affecting them. Select committees would be the forum for processing these petitions and will make recommendations to the full House.

Incidentally, there are a variety of ways in which the first cycle could be started – tossing a coin, 'hide haan behine back', the short straw, mutual consent etc. Despite appearances, this is not to trivialise something of immense importance. But since all will have prizes in the end, does it really matter how the race to development is started, providing it is free and fair? Moreover, the practice of appointing people to public office by lottery has respectable origins. The Athenian democrats from the fifth to the third centuries BC did this as a means of ensuring political equality.[43] If the political elite cannot decide, because real political acts are always difficult for that select group, then the people should be the final arbiters on method. I would argue against the use of the electoral means to determine who has first turn because of a fear of the mother of all political battles; the collateral damage from which might destroy everything at the first hurdle. In the end it has to be left to dialogue and the constitution designers: though common sense would suggest that the PNCR should start the process if only because the PPP/C have formed the government since the return of free and fair elections in 1992. A break from battle fatigue could provide a real opportunity to recharge and function more effectively in five years time.

The main purpose for writing this section is to suggest an alternative to the grand coalition as the means to power sharing and good governance in a deeply divided society. That alternative is the rotating five year term of party government with the possibility of extension to ten years in time. The latter would be dependent on the judgement and recommendations of the Constitution Reform Commission (CRC) and the approval of the people. It is assumed that the CRC would remain a permanent monitoring commission and would deal with changes in political culture and party realignments as they become significant. Because nothing ever stays the same, this Commission becomes the important tracking system for social change and the demands it makes for adjustments in the way the country organises its political, social and economic life. The initial details of how such a government is to be organised and run are already in the existing constitution and its proposed adjustments. These include the select committees and their functions, the commissions covering large aspects of human relationships, the provision for dispute resolution, the operations and responsibilities of a government in waiting and the provision of access to participation for minorities.

The programme and focus of each government would be taken from the existing and generally agreed National Development Strategy. The targets would be publicly agreed before the start of each term by Parliament and the technical experts who monitor the implementation of the development programme. This is the heart of the change. From now on the struggle is not to be directed at power acquisition. It is to be the cooperative use of power in the pursuit of human development. A development committee to oversee the overall workings of such radical change should be instituted. Part of their mandate should be to report and recommend to Parliament at regular intervals on the workings of the programme. Such a committee could either be international, drawn from the great and the good of Guyana, or a mixture of both. It is profoundly important that the reasons for such a radical change of focus and action are explained to the people and that they are then given the opportunity to choose before fundamental changes are implemented in their name. They should be clear in their minds that from here on political power is to be harnessed to development for all and not in the service of any particular group. That there will be disagreements is true, but in time the debates which take place will be less partisan, based on honest information, and thoughtful choices. Guyana, its citizens and its people would be well on the way to arriving.

I want to spend the rest of this section explaining the principles which underpin my preference for time-limited, rotating government over grand coalition. Following John Burton and his colleagues in Conflict Resolution I have argued elsewhere[44] that all human beings have certain existential needs which must be satisfied if social order is to be maintained. These needs are for security, both physical and psychological, for the right to participate in the total life of one's community, recognition of one's human identity and the dignity which goes with it, and distributive justice. Taken together they make up the need of individuals and groups to have some control over their lives.

And so, in a society such as Guyana, the satisfaction of this need for control has to involve, in my view, constitutionally determined regular access to power and authority for each of the main groups. It will not come out of majoritarian politics. Nor will it come out of sharing on the basis of the grand coalition, mutual vetoes and proportionality, since this presumes a degree of willingness on the part of elites to cooperate and solve problems. This does not exist today, and will not arrive by magic. Alternating government with a government in waiting and the cooperation it invites might very well encourage those values of understanding and trust which might make some other form of power sharing work at a later date.

Need satisfaction does not have to be absolute. Approximations will do, providing it is the best which can be achieved, it is done with fairness, and the satisfaction boundaries are constantly being pushed back, i.e., the implementation of the national development plan is being pursued with relentless vigour. Failure, over time, to satisfy these needs could lead to public protest, strikes, and eventually to violence.

There is no necessary hierarchy in these needs. They are all intimately interdependent and interlinked. The need for participation is to be highlighted here because it means inclusion and promises fairness in distribution, recognition of identity and therefore security. Now, we know that for the last thirty-eight years a phenomenal amount of human energy and physical resources have been squandered in the struggle for control in the expectation that at least one group will have their needs satisfied. This has failed miserably. Instead, the expenditure has bought insecurity, exclusion, misrecognition, unfairness, and the loss of dignity for all. At a stroke, however, the legal right to power and responsibility that comes with alternating government and government in waiting, transfers the struggle for power into the struggle for development. Giving political power to race now diffuses the power of race to infect politics. All have the opportunity to become engaged for welfare and not for supremacy. Elsewhere,[45] I have dealt with village government as the second half of the principle of engagement.

Throughout this book I have been celebrating the eventual growth of the people as thoughtful citizens, emancipated from fears of racial domination. This I have chosen to call Participatory Democracy. According to Charles Taylor,[46] the minimum requirements are:

- A unity of purpose among its peoples. This does not mean total agreement but a set of common goals which provide focus for open debate and considered choice.
- That its citizens are treated equally and
- That the society is prepared to deliver on its obligations to its members.

The NDS and its five yearly programmes should satisfy the demands for debate and choice, while rotating governments should provide for equality and fairness.

I put forward this view of power sharing as a part of the debate. It concentrates on broad principles and makes no claims to absolute truth. It could be deemed an overenthusiastic view of human rationality. That might be so. The alternatives seem to me to be complex, hemmed in by the threat of vetoes. They present a picture of people in a room continuously looking over their shoulders. This does not make for cooperation and trust and does nothing for the growth of citizenship and a Guyanese people.

My sole intention in the second half of this chapter is to offer a solution to the problem of 'periodic changes of government' in a deeply divided society. Inevitably, a proposition as novel as sharing political power in a time-limited, alternating form will raise many questions. Many of these invite speculation about the nature and direction of change in human affairs. Accuracy in this prediction is not possible, but the papers by the PNCR, the PPP/C and David Hinds give clear indications of the institutional provisions which could be made to handle the rate and burden of change as they arise. Select committees, public service commissions, oversight committees for the constitution, national development objectives and the protection of minorities are all set up to ensure accountability, to monitor change, and to advise Parliament on how adjustments to these changes might be made.

I will however, attempt to deal briefly with two questions. These are:

1. Can alternating government be democratic?
2. Is this not likely to further institutionalise ethnicity in Guyanese public life?

1. In keeping with their historical, cultural and ideological convictions, democracies can be organised and run in a variety of ways. We therefore have to be careful not to confuse democratic principles with their institutional forms. Some of these principles are:

-   that government should be representative. There should be free and fair elections at regular intervals on an adult suffrage;
-   that government should be legitimate. That is, it should have the consent of the governed;
-   that government should be accountable, not only at election time, but throughout its life. Significant public matters should be discussed and debated widely before decisions are made. This is widespread participation in action;
-   that the rule of law should prevail, and
-   that there should be periodic changes of government by peaceful means.

Institutions which enshrine the above principles are democratic. Behaviour which sets out to make those principles work for the benefit of all the people is democratic politics in motion. Working democracies, the world over, have designed their institutions in keeping with the antecedent conditions mentioned at the start of this discussion. British democracy expresses itself differently from the American, even though they are both majoritarian examples. Their cabinets are composed and run differently, so are their legislatures, electoral systems and supreme courts. These are different again from the Belgian and Dutch which are consensus forms and share executive power, use proportional representation for their electoral systems and whose legislatures and supreme courts function differently. New Zealand, Finland, India and Ireland among others, also have variations in their institutions but none would doubt their claims to being working democracies

But these are not the only possible institutional arrangements. Countries, especially postcolonial ones, with significant ethnic divisions, need to fashion their institutions from the foundations up and in keeping with their own historical and cultural inheritances. In this sense, constitutionally determined, time-limited, alternating government, satisfies the criterion of periodic change which ethnically driven winner-takes-all elections will not do. It removes the fear of losing and its consequences. It restores to each group the pride and dignity which comes with the opportunities to participate fully in the life of their country. It removes the generators of conflict.

Is all this likely to further institutionalise an aggressive ethnicity? Outcomes in human affairs are difficult to predict but if the contention that there is nothing inherently conflictual in ethnicity, then I think not. If cooperation replaces conflict then it matters not whether the boundaries remain intact or become more permeable. We must remember this, throughout all the troubles, there has been good neighbourliness, peaceful coexistence, love and partnerships between the groups, and Guyana's mixed population continues to grow.

Summary.

I am attempting to argue throughout this work for a liberated multi-ethnic postcolonial society. Liberation means the transition from subjecthood, to citizenship, to a Guyanese people. Subjecthood is the state of existence where rules and decisions are imposed from above and enforced by coercion. Citizenship evolves when these subjects are given the opportunity to make or participate in the making of those decisions which affect their lives and welfare. I am not thinking about those four or five yearly acts of voting but real opportunities for self-development which come with the challenges to think beyond narrow interests to the greater common good, be it at local or national levels. Of course, there will still be disagreements but in the reconstructed society there will be means to deal with them. Realising that this actively collaborating citizen will not arrive by magic I set out to demonstrate in Chapter Two one set of engagements that will nurture this liberation from the grass roots up. In the current chapter I have extended the real opportunities for engagement beyond the local to the national.

At the end of this painstaking and challenging process must be the expectation of an essentially Guyanese working democracy, a peaceful and fair society engaged in its own development and the recognisable stirrings of a Guyanese people. None of this will arrive on the backs of old political habits and behaviour. The politics of power required a certain selfishness and ruthlessness in its behavioural baggage. The public purse was unashamedly for private gain. The new politics of collaboration and consensus need to be guided by values of cooperation, honesty, respect, fairness and unhampered participation. The public purse must be for the public good. This means a revolution in institutional and political behaviour of politicians and people. The remainder of this book will deal with one further aspect of this massive need for change. This is leadership.

END NOTES

1. Hinds, D. (2001), 'Race Democracy and Power Sharing' www.guyanacaribbeanpolitics.com/commentary.
2. Ibid., p.3.
3. Ibid.,p. 5.
4. Ibid., p.4.
5. Ibid., p.4.
6. Ibid., pp 3-4.
7. Ibid., p.5. and Kwayana, E. (2001) 'Common sense about power sharing.' www.guyanacaribbeanpolitics.com
8. Ibid., p.7.
9. Lijphart, A. (1968), The *Politics of Accommodation: Pluralism and Democracy in the Netherlands, Berkeley*, CA, University of California Press.
10. Lijphart, A. (1988), 'Citation Classic, No. 39', www.garfield.library. upenn.classics1988
11. Lijphart, A. (1999), 'Power-Sharing and Group Autonomy in the 1990's and the 21st. Century,' Constitutional Design, 2000, San Diego, University of California.
12. Lijphart, A. (1991), 'The Power-Sharing Approach,' in Montville, J. V. (ed.), (1991), *Conflict and Peacemaking in Multi-ethnic Societies,* New York, Macmillan, pp. 494-95.
13. McRae, K. D. (1991), 'Theories of Power-Sharing and Conflict Management,' in Montville, J. V. (ed.), (1991), *Conflict and Peacemaking in Multiethnic Societies,* New York, Macmillan, pp. 93-97.
14. Hinds, (2001), p. 7.
15. Ibid., p. 11.
16. Ibid., pp. 12-14. The rest of this section is based on these pages,
17. Ibid., p. 8.
18. In the 2001 elections the PNC obtained 41.8% of votes cast; by 2006 this had fallen to 34%. See Guyana News and Information – Past election results (www.guyana.org/Elections/ past_results.html)
19. www.guyanacaribbeanpolitics.com 6.12.2002.
20. PNCR (2002), *Shared Governance*, p.1.
210. Ibid., p.2.
22. Ibid., pp 2-7.
23. Ibid., p. 1.

24. Ibid., p. 2.
25. Ibid., pp. 2-7
26. Ibid., p 5.
27. www.guyanacaribbeanpolitics.com 'Try power sharing in parliament first' – Jagdeo. Posted 30. 01. 03 by Patrick Denny.
28. Ibid., 'Building Trust To Achieve Genuine Political Co-operation.' Presented by the PPP/C Government. Posted 11. 02. 03.
29. Ibid.
30. Ibid., p. 1.
31. Ibid., p. 2.
32. Ibid., p. 5
33. Ibid., p. 4
34. Lijphart, A. (1991), 'The Power-Sharing Approach,' in Montville, J.V. ed. (1991), Conflict and *Peacemaking in Multiethnic Societies,* New York, Lexington Books, p. 500.
35. Ibid., p. 497.
36. Ibid., p. 500.
37. Ibid., p. 500-501.
38. See International Labour Organisation, SAP 2.84/WP.143, 'Structural adjustment and agriculture in Guyana: From Crisis to recovery'. Available online at *www.ilo.org/public/english/dialogue/sector/papers/agrguyan/index.htm*
39. Mitrany, D. (1946*), A Working Peace System,* Chicago, Quadrangle p. 36.
40. www.guyanacaribbeanpolitics.com See submissions by David Hinds, Eusi Kwayana, PNC/R, Tara Singh and Dhanpaul Narine and others.
41. Sites, P. (1973), *Control, The Basis of Social Order,* New York, Dunellen Publishing Co.
42. Euben, P. J. (2001), 'The Polis, Globalisation, and the Politics of Place', in Botwinick. A. and Connolly, W. E. (2001), *Democracy and Vision,* Princeton, Princeton University Press, p.259.
43. Honohan, I. (2001), 'Freedom as citizenship: The Republican Tradition in Political Theory' in *The Republic,* Dublin, p. 8.
44. Seecoomar, J. (2002), *Contributions Towards The Resolution of Conflict in Guyana,* Peepal Tree Press, Leeds, Chap. Six.
45. See Chapter Two of the current work.
46. Taylor, C. (2000), 'Foreword,' in Gagnon, A-G, and Tilly, J. (eds), *Multinational Democracies,* Cambridge, CUP.

CHAPTER FOUR

LEADERSHIP.

In the Preface to Volume 1 of *The Open Society And Its Enemies,* Sir Karl Popper warns us not to defer uncritically to our great men and women. For, he says, "Great men may make great mistakes,"[1] sometimes with horrendous consequences. It would therefore be tempting to begin this chapter with a historical resumé of political leadership in Guyana since the 1950s. This would certainly help us to understand our confused condition, but such an account would inevitably be critical and could be taken as part of the culture of blame which passes for political discourse. Additionally, in today's Guyana, criticism is often interpreted as bias, and so the exercise might aggravate rather than help to solve difficulties. Our leaders were awarded the accolade of greatness even in their own lifetimes and within that select group they certainly made great blunders. I do not intend to undertake that critique here. It is a task which Guyanese scholarship will have to confront with openness and honesty,[2] lest "by our reluctance to criticise some of it, we may help to destroy it all." Worth mentioning, though, are Tyrone Ferguson's study of the Burnham years, *To Survive Sensibly or to Court Heroic Death: Management of Guyana's Political Economy 1965-1985,* and Clem Seecharan's *Sweetening Bitter Sugar, Jock Campbell, the Booker Reformer in British Guiana, 1934-1966*[3]. In the first, one of the architects of Desmond Hoyte's period of 'structural adjustment' between 1985-1992, attempts a balanced assessment of the achievements and failures of the Burnham years. Whilst Guyanese critics of Ferguson's study such as Freddie Kissoon[4] acknowledge its usefulness in recognising the immensity of the task that the first independent government faced in terms of the economic and administrative legacy of colonialism, Kissoon criticises

Ferguson's study precisely because it does not deal with the extraordinarily individualised style of leadership that characterised Burnham's years in power, still less with the role of Burnham's charismatic personality in shaping the style and nature of that leadership role. In the absence of a scholarly biography of Forbes Burnham, the tendency has been for bizarre fragments of myth to accrete around a legendary space. Several works of fiction have suggested the lineaments that a biography would have to investigate, such as Pauline Melville's short story, 'The President's Exile' in her collection, *The Migration of Ghosts*,[5] where Baldwin Hercules, a figure with unmistakeable resemblances to Burnham, revisits his past in the moments of dying as the result of a throat operation. He is last seen riding his spectral white horse around Georgetown. There is also Lakshmi Persaud's novel, *For the Love of My Name* (2000)[6] which attempts to get inside the psyche of a Burnham like figure and again make use of some well recognised 'incidents' where truth may well be stranger than fiction and have all the power of cautionary myth. A work of scholarly biography would need to separate truth from myth, without losing sight of the fact that the myths had a powerful reality; it would need to confront the relationship between the presidential personality and the nature of Guyanese political culture to begin to explain how political institutions could be bent so readily towards an autocratic will.

Echoing in some respects Ferguson's contrast between heroic vision and political reality, Clem Seecharan's very detailed biography of Jock Campbell, the chairman of Bookers, who instituted a very practical reform programme to improve conditions on the sugar estates, portrays the role of Cheddi Jagan in a generally unflattering light. The practical reformer is contrasted with the ideologue, with a 'purity of motives and an incorrigible naivety',[7] whose political antennae for what was possible in a given situation Seecharan sees as sadly lacking. There is some suggestive but sketchy rooting of these characteristics in biography, with an attempt to explain some of Dr. Jagan's alleged shortcomings as a politician in terms of an absence of particular kinds of cultural reference, but there is clearly a need for a thorough political biography that is neither hagiographic nor dismissive of his real virtues. In Seecharan's study, Jagan is seen very much as the architect of his own, his party's, and the Guyanese people's misfortunes. A study that examines his leadership style and personal strengths and weaknesses in the context of leading the PPP for almost fifty years is long overdue.

It is abundantly evident that some of the features of Guyanese political leadership are by no means unique to Guyana. As early as 1968, A.W. Singham's *The Hero and the Crowd in a Colonial Polity*[8] had in its study of the political career of Eric Gairy in Grenada, identified the wider tendency in Caribbean politics for authoritarianism to characterise the relationship between leader and party, government and people and between the political elite and the working class.

Singham's work was refined further in countless papers by the Trinidadian political economist Lloyd Best, and characterised by the unforgettable term of 'doctor politics'. Best's analysis (see in particular, 'From Chaguaramas to Slavery'[9]) relates in particular to what Gordon Rohlehr has described as the 'egocentric authoritarianism' of Dr Eric Williams in Trinidad. Best looks closely, for instance, at the role of colonial education is shaping the self-conceptions of a whole generation of Caribbean political leaders. Both Singham and Best offer Guyanese scholars useful theoretical foundations for the study of Guyana's special contributions to 'egocentric authoritarianism'.

But while the writer with an unashamed peacemaking agenda must tread a thin line, since the tendency is inevitably to see criticism of leaders as motivated by ethnic loyalties, the people cannot be bound by any such constraints. In a set of interviews for an earlier study,[10] the recurring lament of respondents was that in their naked personal ambition, and their uncompromising lust for power, politicians had corrupted a relatively peaceful society. Politicians, and in particular political leaders, had succeeded in spreading a disturbing uncertainty, suspicion and fear throughout the land in order to ensure that their supporters stayed on side. They did not hesitate to encourage envy, jealousy and doubts and so set group against group. They lacked vision about the good society and, in particular, how it might be achieved.[11] This is not to say that Guyana's political leaders have lacked vision in the sense of having a goal of a transformed postcolonial society. Forbes Burnham's idea of the co-operative as the core Guyanese political unit could be seen as a brave and worthwhile experiment were it not for the factors which inevitably undermined it – the all-centralising power of the state, the play of ethnic politics, and the corruption of the political elite to the point where the acquisition of power and the recognition it conferred on them seem to have become the compelling motivational force. The vision of the good society had to have at its centre a very different conception of the relationship between leadership and the whole Guyanese people. This is what, in their own words, some of the people said:

> **Respondent:** ...As a teacher I feel that I had no problem. I taught both races – the two major races I am speaking about. As a teacher I found I could not be racial.
>
> In Georgetown, we did not have too many problems until 1963, when I think it was politics that caused all the racial problems we experienced. In those days I lived in Regent Street which was already becoming a commercial area, and I saw lots of things happening there. I saw them trying to beat the Indian out of the Dougla, the Black out of the Dougla. To me the Dougla suffered more...
>
> As I mentioned, I feel that the politicians, whether consciously or unconsciously, have used race to divide our country. And that is my personal opinion.
>
> **Interviewer:** Why do you think the politicians did that?
>
> **Resp.:** I am not sure I can answer that, but let me try. You see, although both major parties claim to be multiracial, we feel that it is just window dressing. The PPP do have some black faces, but not in any large numbers and vice versa for the PNC. I feel that deep down, those two parties are basically Black or Indian.
>
> Why they should want to promote this race thing, I really don't know. It is a case of divide and rule again – the old, old system. Because what I remember reading – the whole race question goes back long before '63. I wasn't aware of it then.
>
> After '63 it eased up again, but that period was very painful. My friends from the countryside tell me that the kind of close relationships that Blacks and Indians had were totally lost after the '63 problem. And why I say it was the politicians? It was not the villagers themselves who were upset with their neighbours. It became bigger than them. The parties said so. In some cases they had to move house and go into other areas. Not because they had a problem with their black neighbours but because the

politicians made it a huge political problem...

Interview No. 55. 06. 08. 97.

(A Mixed Guyanese woman in her late 40s)

Int.: ...what would you suggest might be done to get a greater degree of harmony than currently exists in the society?
Resp. Working backwards, from symptom to cause I would say that the political question – that politics inflames racial tensions to the point that it comes above the surface. Politics brings it up, fosters it, encourages it and plays on the power insecurities which end up being racial insecurities because there is a Black party and an Indian party... I don't care what they say, they might try as much as possible to use the ideology, to use policies and manifestos – the bottom line is the appeal to the racial factor and how much the appeal to that racial factor is. It is a measure of the desperation. I can't begin to emphasise enough how much these two parties contribute to the inflaming of what's already there...

Interview No. 59. 11. 08. 97.

(An Indian Guyanese man in his 30s)

Resp.: ...There is absolutely no reason why two or three sets of people of different historical or cultural backgrounds should not be able to live in peace and harmony together. In this regard I think our track record has been good and fairly stable except for a few eruptions we have had from time to time.

This would bring one to the base of these eruptions which I would say were based mainly on politics. It was politics which tended to divide the two basic ethnic groups. The major parties used the racial factor as the base for their operations.

I think that it was a happy augury for the country that the PPP when it was first established was a united group, bringing together the major racial groups in this country. I think that was a most significant change. And just as significant as it was an achievement, it was equally significant when the party split and divided. I prayed, I begged and hoped that it wouldn't take place. But it did take place. And the fact that each group was led by a person of a certain ethnic origin and that their main base and support was of their own ethnic following, that exacerbated the problem. And since 1955 we have had serious problems, and a racial front exploding into riots, commotion and disturbances in this country... Yet at the same time the thing is contradictory because I believe that the ordinary man/woman, the working class man or woman at the bottom there – they have an affinity. They have a closeness which people don't realise that they have, a common interest which isn't used to bring them closer together. Instead external forces came into play and separation got in...

Interview No. 58 11.08.97.

(An African Guyanese man in his 70s)

In a book which seeks to look forward, the concentration must be on the qualities, guides and actions which must come from our leaders if we are to move from behaviours which promote conflict to those which encourage cooperation in our political and social relationships. Power politics exudes a certain aggressive style which our leaders provided in abundance, but which failed to produce the much-wanted Cooperative Republic. (There is probably no need to document this style in depth, but the last four decades of Guyana's politics can provide too many examples of triumphalist marches of ethnic assertion, violent street demonstrations, the brutal break-up of peaceful demonstrations – not to mention the shocking incidence of political assassinations during the Burnham years.) It is a style driven by the desire to win and hold power and to benefit clients and supporters. In any form of sharing, the responsibilities of governing Guyana, the old approaches will fail. Leadership must now set out to benefit all in a deliberate and transparent effort. It requires a mind set which moves from a belief that political power confers unassailable rights to act narrowly, to one which "focuses more on human needs [and their satisfaction for all], reasoning, and collaborative problem solving. [This] is a dramatic paradigm shift,"[12] which like so much else in post colonial governance requires deliberate and persistent acts of thought, cooperative action and imagination, to make it work.

In another idiom such a monumental task requires scales to fall as they did to Saul on the way to Damascus. This is not to make a special plea to God to send us a special consignment of Guyanese leaders devoid of all sin! It is to demand leadership which takes seriously the stimulus of ideas for the general good, the design of institutions and the irrepressible will to make them work for all.

Leaders in the consensus frame therefore require humility, flexibility and keen insight as part of their intellectual baggage. Humility, to recognise that postcolonial societies like Guyana are complex, too little understood and the obvious taken too much for granted. They are complex because of their manufactured cultural and ethnic structure. They are too little understood because there have not been enough serious efforts made to probe their internal dynamics. Studies such as those by Leo Depres and R.A. Glasgow were made over fifty years ago within a theoretical framework[13] – that of 'cultural pluralism' – that itself requires radical overhaul. The obvious that is in danger of being the taken-for-granted is the kind of ethnic stasis that the pluralist thesis tends to see as a fixed political reality. Guyanese need the kind of scholarship that is sensitive to the dynamics of change, the undercurrents of ethnic relationships outside the corral of tribal politics. Brackette F. Williams' *Stains on My Name, War in My Veins: Guyana and the Politics of Cultural Struggle*[15] is certainly an interesting attempt to make sense of the play between fluidity and apparent fixities in Guyanese ethnic identities. Very pertinently Williams reminds us that within the general labels of 'African' and 'Indian' Guyanese there are in reality very considerable diversities of cultural identity. Williams also argues persuasively that whatever the reality of competition and conflict, there is also a process of homogenisation towards a common Guyanese identity taking place, even though ethnic identities and a core of cultural practices remain distinct for each group.

Nevertheless, there remains an awesome challenge to Guyanese scholarship to undertake the kind of studies that will allow us to truly understand ourselves. Only on the basis of such an understanding can we devise social arrangements which are legitimately suited to our needs.

In 2005, thirty-nine years after independence, the majority of Guyanese are still subjects. They are still prevented from being active citizens who are involved in their own development and welfare.[15] Decisions are made for them by the party. They still have to obey. What passes for public debate is largely the party line and 'divide and rule' is as raw as it has ever been. Our post-independence leaders were either seduced by the trappings of colonial rule or got lost in a sea of confused ideological thinking. Deliberate acts to transform the people into active citizens and eventually into a Guyanese people, do not appear to have been in their thoughts let alone on their political agendas.[16]

How then can our leaders acquire the qualities of humility

and flexibility which are necessary for consensus politics and which are anathema to the power game?

Before I go on, I want to return to what I consider to be the greatest error of our early leaders and its destructive consequences. That is their abandonment of the nation-building enterprise in the second half of the 1950s, nearly a decade before political independence. I believe that the division into competing ethnic segments was not inevitable. If there were genuine ideological differences between the rival sections, they were not insuperable, as the direction of post-independence politics revealed. What is difficult to believe is that the rival leaderships were unaware of the ethnic and wider social implications of their actions. What is manifest is a style of leadership that was unable to compromise in the interests of the people, that treated political parties as fiefdoms through which to exercise control. Instead of nation-building, the political leaderships chose the vain pursuit of exclusive, partisan power in order to control the state, its resources and their distributions for the benefit of one section of the population. The consequences we know. The conclusion must be that any leadership which favours one section of the population is never likely to win widespread approval. It leads inexorably to the aggressive defence of the indefensible and to a politics of confusion

The enduring and most horrific legacy of this abandonment was that at independence Guyana moved smoothly out of the embrace of one colonial master into the arms of home-grown substitute. For whilst our leaders were militantly anti-colonial, they did not set out to transform what was at the core of the culture of colonialism – the power relations between ruler and ruled. On the contrary, they adopted it with gusto. Race and party now became the new divide and rule and the overwhelming number of the people remained subjects and denied the role of participative citizen.

Let me also put to rest once again the excuse that ethnic mix means inevitable conflict. Significant sections of the Guyanese political intelligentsia and the people have always debunked the idea and have done so in the vein of Claude Ake the Nigerian political economist who said:

The problem is not ethnicity but bad leadership. There is nothing conflictual about ethnic differences. They lead to strife only when they are politicised and it is the elites who politicise ethnicity in their quest for power and support. Leaders also gain a second advantage from exploiting ethnicity. Having incited ethnic based conflict, they can then use the threat of such conflict to justify political authoritarianism.[17]

Leadership for the politics of power demands aggression, especially when on the defensive.[18] It demands centralised control of decision and action, coercion, keeping the people in bondage by denying them access to reasoned choices. It is a leadership characterised by inflexibility, and the absence of humility. Such leaders always have to claim the prerogative of right because to admit error, or that someone else might have a worthwhile idea, would be an unbearable sign of weakness. Leaders addicted to political power find being without it intolerable. They will stop at nothing to regain it. As has been too common in Guyana, a bullying politics is transferred to the streets. Disruption and sabotage become commonplace. And all this is done in order to gain the upper hand over the existing government in order to be able to negotiate from strength.[19] This leaves a monumental mismatch between the demands of democracy and its institutions and the reality of non democratic politics.

Now, a change from gladiatorial to consensus politics will need profoundly different leadership talents, abilities, and approaches. The focus changes from power for its own sake to shared power in the service of the people, their welfare and their development. This movement of the people centre stage means making them available for participation in their own growth, and so decision-making has to be consultative and collaborative and dedicated to the resolution of human problems. It is in accepting the participation of the people that leaders most need to be humble and flexible.

Aspects of Leadership for the Consensus Frame.

In the remainder of this chapter I want to deal with aspects of the demands that any redesigned set of democratic institutions will make on leadership, if it is to produce a politics of sharing, inclusion, genuine internal dialogue at all levels, and thus a working multi-ethnic democracy.

Leaders in this mould need to be problem-oriented. They need to be managers of change in an environment which generates perpetual change. Their primary concern would be to encourage the growth of a culture of governance which has problem-solving at its core. Such a leadership would focus on the identification of problems and their analysis. And in doing this, engage with all the knowledge, expertise and variety of interpretations which are available. It would also relentlessly pursue clarity and precision in definition and the careful examination of options, together with their human and physical costs, before making choices for their solutions. It is here that creativity, vision, and boldness, have the opportunity to permeate politics. It is here, also, that public debate and criticism can have their greatest effects in preventing large-scale error and avoidable human costs.

Leaders in this problem-solving vein will be attuned to monitoring policy implementation and the functioning of institutions with great care to detect failure or unintended consequence, to rethink and to reformulate solutions and try again. They will know that failure is not evil, nor is its admission a sign of weakness. Failures are only discarded approximations to truth. It is learning from our errors which makes for the growth of knowledge and understanding and therefore for more creative approaches to our problems

In this frame, the leader, stripped of all his/her (their) pretensions to omnipotence, is the arch facilitator, the person who cannot have all the knowledge but is able to recognise talent and harness its capabilities in a collaborative enterprise for the social good. S/he will have the vision and creative imagination to design consensual social policies for the present and future welfare of all the people and will be capable of handling dissent evenhandedly and communicating effectively. A leader who strives after consensus will be someone who is flexible and mentally agile and who realises that the success of the cooperative state depends on this culture of problem solving permeating all institutional life. John Burton concludes, "that an essential quality of leadership in a problem solving frame is more than an ability just to respond to demands, pressures, interests and the views of an electorate. It is an ability to help in defining the goals of the electorate and to arrive at a consensus on policies designed to satisfy the needs of societies, not only now but also in the longer term."[20]

At its best then, democracy as consensus is a lifelong learning and educational enterprise for all its citizens. The encouragement to participate made by enlightened leaders, at different levels of decision, would make for a people who are thoughtful, concerned, and willing to share in a game of development and social transformation in which all can win. The citizens' sense of inclusion and of having views that are valued are prerequisites for movement along the nation-building road. It requires that most of the citizens are satisfied with the performance of the institutions they have helped to design, are confident that their leaders are accessible and responsive to their needs, that opportunities for advance exist and that no section of the population feels excluded from the benefits of the society. One writer sums up the importance of good leadership thus, "A good leader has the wisdom and political skill to sense the public mood, build consensus, mobilise support, inspire and justify needed sacrifices, marshal resources, attract other good leaders and do whatever is necessary to function effectively.[21]

In arguing for a kinder, more gentle democratic leadership, I am not making a case for weakness. Once the decisions have been arrived at consensually, leaders have to be firm and resolute. Day to day management demands that they be allowed to lead.

Guyana revisited.

At first glance, it does indeed seem to be crying for the moon or the superhuman. This is not so. It is an alternative framework for the management of change and the promotion of progress for all. Forty years of the politics of power have not produced significant movement towards peace or development. It is not likely that more of the same adversarial politics or leadership styles will produce anything different. The cry of utopianism can be tempered also, if we bear in mind that the most important quality of the leader in this mould is being able to harness the available talent and expertise and asking penetrating questions about information, assumptions, analysis and choices. At present, in Guyana, this is not possible because at any one time at least half the skills and abilities are in disaffected opposition and lost to the entire society.

Yet the people want to live peacefully and to have their needs satisfied. They would welcome any set of institutions which hold out real promise for peace and progress. They wish their leaders would talk seriously to each other, design these institutions, and devote their energies to making them work for all. This, instead of legislative cockfights, hurling charges of fraud, deceit, and lies at each other, and encouraging the anarchy of political violence on the streets.

To those members of the elite who find sharing a threat to their monopoly of power, consensus politics is an unbearable burden of change which is to be resisted at any cost. Such an unyielding approach to Guyanese politics holds the country to ransom. It blocks social and economic advance and perpetuates avoidable suffering. Measured against the obligations of being the peoples' representatives it is an unforgivable abuse of power.

A consensual democracy in Guyana requires the steadfast cooperation of leaders across the boundaries once they are convinced that the gaps are bridgeable – and this because they accept that the existing political arrangements generate deadlock and disunity. They have to be prepared to make determined efforts to understand each other's needs and work together to make certain that whatever agreements they arrive at are seen as fair for all. They have to work honestly for the proper functioning of the institutions they design.

Guyanese political leaders must recognise that the people have conferred on them this political and moral responsibility. Until, at least, the elections of 2006, the two largest political parties together have the electoral support of around 90% of the voting population. They also have strong endorsement from their membership to engage in constructive acts of cooperation and change. To pursue a narrower agenda would be to abrogate a sacred responsibility and continue to mock the aspirations of the people.

Summary.

The chapter set out to examine the qualities which any redesigned set of democratic institutions will make on leadership, if they are to produce a politics of sharing and inclusion

Post independence Guyanese leadership, whilst vehemently anti-colonial with respect to the vestiges of metropolitan political and economic power, in their style of governance rapidly embraced the culture of colonialism. It did not set out to transform it, at least not with any great conviction or sustained action. 'Divide and rule' therefore found a ready home in 'race and party.' It continues to this day.

Our leaders must guide the process of liberation from the subjecthood of colonial and racially bound party rule into developing a citizenry in which all are given the opportunity to participate in making decisions. Over time, this engagement might then begin to develop a core set of values which are not sectarian but confront the needs of the whole society. It is the role of good leadership to articulate those values. If we reach this stage, we will have begun to develop into a people; that is, the elusive multi-ethnic nation in which one can be African and Guyanese, Indian and Guyanese and whatever else one wants to be but also truly comfortable with being Guyanese.

In addition to this public vision and acquiring the qualities of humility, flexibility, integrity and honesty, and the will to solve problems collaboratively, our leaders need to be:

- Pursuers of consensus who are responsible and accountable for the welfare and development of all the people;
- Problem solvers and facilitators who use all the talents, abilities and expertise that are available. In doing this, they would create a decision-making environment which is interactive and cooperative;

- Able to admit errors, redesign, and start again without fear of losing face.
- Encouragers of the problem solving approach to decision-making at the local, community, and the executive levels.
- Attentive listeners and effective communicators who take seriously the need for two-way communication in policy making and its implementation.
- Able to design institutions that satisfy the needs of all the people, and accept the need for checks and balances on their power.
- Committed not to use power for selfish or partisan ends.

It is worth repeating that if a nation is to be built in a divided society, leaders across the divide will have to cooperate to solve the problems of the whole society and not be hemmed in by the demands of their sectional constituencies. Part of this process means a willingness to explain and educate those who look to them for leadership and to invite public discussion and debate about the reasons for policy choices.

Without these changes, can we be sure our country will not disintegrate? There is too much evidence around the world that states are perfectly capable of failing. In the midst of Guyana's darkest times, the novelist Pauline Melville was drawn to imagine just that fate. In her novel, *The Ventriloquist's Tale*, one of her characters, Ollie Sampson, the finance minister, has the fantasy of getting to his feet at the United Nations and declaring:

> Ladies and Gentlemen, I should like to inform you, on behalf of the nation state of Guyana, that we are going to resign from being a country. We can't make it work. We have tried. We have done our best. It is not possible. The problems are insoluble. From midnight tonight, we shall cease trading. The country is now disbanded. We will voluntarily liquidate ourselves. The nation will disperse quietly, a little shamefaced but so what. We had to go...[22]

Those dark days may have passed, but who could declare, hand on heart, that they could not return.

END NOTES

1. Popper, K. R. (1945), *The Open Society And Its Enemies*, 'Preface to the First Edition', p vii, London, Routledge.
2. Some of this assessment has already started. See for instance: Chase, A. (1994), *Guyana; A Nation in Transit, Burnham's Role*, Georgetown, Pavnikpress; Ferguson, T. (1995), *Structural Adjustment and Good Governance: The Case of Guyana*, Georgetown, Guyana National Printers.
3. Ferguson, T. (1999), *To Survive Sensibly or to Court Heroic Death: Management of Guyana's Political Economy 1965-1985*, Georgetown, Guyana National Printers; Seecharan, C. (2004), *Sweetening Bitter Sugar*, Kingston, Ian Randle Publishers.
4. *Stabroek News*, August 3, 1999
5. London, Bloomsbury Publishing, 1998; 1999 paperback ed. pp 1-25.
6. Leeds, Peepal Tree Press, 2000.
7. *Sweetening Bitter Sugar*, p. 204.
8. New Haven, Conn: Yale University Press, 1968.
9. *New World Quarterly* 2.1 (1965):
10. Seecoomar, J. (2002), *Contributions towards the Resolution of Conflict in Guyana*, Leeds, Peepal Tree Press.
11. This is especially so after the breakdown of the dream of a unified socialist Guyana during the 1950s. Ethnic politics, its divisions and conflicts rushed in to fill the vacuum. After independence (1966), the Prime Minister, L.F.S. Burnham (PNC), proclaimed his vision of liberation for the small man and the development of the country, through a revitalised cooperative movement. By 1979, the cooperative movement had failed and state capitalism was taking over.

    Soon after the PPP came to power in 1992, the Prime Minister, Dr Cheddi Jagan, reaffirmed that his party remained faithful to its Marxist beliefs. He stopped short however, of announcing a Marxist blueprint for Guyana. Since the breakdown of the idea of the cooperatives, the country has been without a publicly stated philosophy for the general good. Within the last five years, however, the political parties have been giving serious consideration to power sharing as a means to inclusive governance. Their thoughts are in the public domain and all Guyana expects that serious discussion and negotiation will bring a breakout of the current deadlock.

12. Burton, J. W. (1997), *Violence Explained,* Manchester, Manchester University Press, p. 14. This chapter relies heavily on this work. As usual the entire book is saturated with Burtonian thinking.

13. Depres, Leo, *Cultural Pluralism and Nationalist Politics in British Guiana*, Chicago, Rand McNally, 1967; and Glasgow, R.A., *Guyana: Race and Politics Among Africans and East Indians*, Hague, Nijhoff, 1970.

14. Durham, Duke University Press, 1991; see especially pp 251-271.

15. Local Government and Proportional Representation are two illustrations of this point. Before independence, local control of local life was embryonic and inadequate but the people took pride in the little they were allowed to manage. Independence brought regional organisation. Staffed and controlled from the centre, even the few opportunities which the people had for participation were taken away from them. This did not only deprive them of the right to some control over their lives, it robbed them of the opportunities to grow as confident and cooperating citizens. (See the peoples' lamentations in Chap. 2 of this work.)

    Proportional Representation was introduced in 1964 with the sole purpose of removing one party from government. As a by-product, it also undermined the nature of representative government. Voting for party lists instead of constituency representatives, the people were again deprived – this time of identifiable MP's. This removes that dynamic relationship between representative and constituent and undermines the whole notion of accountability. The need to consult an MP now becomes a convoluted process of seeking a favour instead of a right.

16. In Guyanese life, an effective demonstration of power politics as tight control, domination and eventual failure, is enshrined in the doctrine of 'party paramountcy'. In 1974 the leader of the PNC declared that from then on the affairs of state would be subordinated to the demands of the party. This meant that there would be direct intervention into the workings of the great institutions of state – the judiciary, church, civil service, the armed forces, the public media and trade unions, – among others. It also meant that since, at its height, the state controlled 80% of salaried jobs, the party could now demand open support

in exchange for employment. To this, add constitutional manipulation and electoral control, and the party in government became unassailable. The leader now became President for life with unlimited executive powers.

The disastrous effects of this widespread politicisation on life in Guyana is best summed up by the Caribbean Conference of Churches, In their 1991 report, they wrote, "The overall conclusion that we came to after a most searching survey of the situation in the Cooperative Republic of Guyana is that this country has, after a series of perhaps well-meaning but certainly unsuccessful political adventures and social experiments, arrived at breaking point in its evolution. The pervasive sense of alienation and of dehumanisation which we discerned knows no social or political limits. All Guyana is affected."

For a more detailed study of leadership during this post independence period, see Seecoomar (2002), especially Chapter 4. See also Ferguson (1995) and (1999), Chase, (1991) and Caribbean Conference of Churches, (1991), 'Report', Bridgetown, Barbados.

17. Ake, C. (1991), 'Rethinking African Democracy,' *Journal of Democracy,* Vol.2. No.1 Winter 1991 pp.32-44

18. The leader of the PNC when faced with determined opposition to his growing authoritarianism retreated behind the support of the armed forces and promised to meet 'steel with more highly tempered steel'. His style of leadership did not allow any other solutions to the disastrous consequences of his policies. For a more detailed study of Guyanese leadership during this period (1966-1985), see Seecoomar, (2002), Chapter Four.

19. See Chapter One of this work for more on the politics of the street and making Guyana ungovernable as leadership aims.

20. Burton, J. (1997), *Violence Explained*, Manchester, Manchester University Press, pp 63-66.

21. Richardson, J.M. (1993), 'Designing Democratic Institutions To Meet The Challenges Of Development', American University, Washington, D.C., p 10.

22. *The Ventriloquist's Tale*, London, Bloomsbury Publishing, 1997, paperback ed. 1998, p. 325

CHAPTER FIVE

CONCLUSION.

In an earlier work[1] I argued that the theoretical framework of human needs and their satisfaction contributed towards an increased understanding of the nature of conflict in communally divided societies. I also claimed that it provided a guide to action for the management of social change, the opportunity for growth in participative democracy and development in its widest sense. For reasons of space, no demonstration of how those claims could be met was possible. This book is an attempt to remedy that defect. It concentrates on the liberation which comes with inclusion and active participation in affairs that matter and the promotion of peace and development It must have been this philosophy of cooperation that those who named Guyana as the Cooperative Republic had in mind.

It begins at the beginning. Ordinary men and women, the so called grassroots, are to be given the responsibility for making choices about their own lives. The intimacy of the village as the base unit comes back to life again and village people are to take part in the growth of their welfare. Local education, health, drainage, sanitation, industry, among a whole range, become their field of operations and decision. Soon however it will become clear that maximum benefit is not possible in very small units. Many villages are too small to support their own secondary schools or health centres, and drainage is not a self-contained problem.

    Village talking to village then becomes a necessity for survival and for progress. Cooperation across boundaries begins to take place. At first hesitant, strictly business; in time comes respect and trust. Larger units come into being and the form of the administrative arrangements changes. Form is function and people-led. It does not come by bureaucratic imposition from above. In this manner webs of collaboration become entrenched. A community begins to be built and dialogue takes the place of destructive protest.

In this dynamic process of local control of local needs, real human benefits emerge. Security grows, identities are recognised and respected, distributive justice begins to happen, conflict loses its *raison d'etre* and lifelong learning takes place. This educational benefit of involvement can be phenomenal. Villagers begin to identify and analyse problems, examine assumptions and evidence, debate, negotiate, persuade and make choices. In monitoring the outcomes of implementation they have to be vigilant and willing to take corrective action if and when it becomes necessary. This exemplifies the power of dialogue and cooperation and so a culture of identifying problems and working towards their resolution develops. It is how knowledge grows. People gain increased access to the powers of their own minds and there can be no greater liberation than this. There is no substitute for direct political experience as a means to the politically educated and engaged citizen because debate, argument, and criticism are fundamental forms of education and a way of developing a sophisticated sense of political judgement which is invaluable in the pursuit of a fairer society.

But local knowledge of local needs has another important contribution to make. It is to the decision making process of a newly transformed, more consensus-oriented central government. A two way traffic of knowledge, information and criticism can make for more sensitive awareness and so for more efficiently targeted political, economic and social action. This marriage of local and central government then becomes a generator of greater inclusion, involvement and 'a people' in a land of 'many peoples'.

On the solid base of decentralised local institutions, we need the foresight and will to foster central political institutions and the conduct of them that nurture and share and include all the people and their representatives in making decisions. The ideas that would underpin these institutions need to recognise that:

- Government and Opposition, as we have known them since independence, have only led to confrontation, adversarial encounters and the stifling of human progress. This is made worse when the divisions are ethnically determined. After 38 years of failure the time has come for change. Institutions must now be designed which promote cooperation and the peaceful management of those conflicts which will inevitably arise.
- The institutional designers must be constantly aware that political representatives hold the welfare of the people in trust. It is therefore the satisfaction of their needs which must be the focus of all institutional activity. Failure to recognise this and act upon it leads to disaffection, polarisation, and destructive conflict.
- A vital part of the culture of governance must be the ability to identify problems and to apply a logical and systematic approach to their solution. The variables of this process – analysis, evidence, debate, costing, choice, monitoring, adjustment – have been discussed before.
- The process of deliberating and deciding together is fundamentally important to the development of trust and a cohesive Guyanese identity. It requires solidarity and commitment towards the aim of political consensus. Without that movement, the nation-building project collapses and the future is bleak indeed.
- Central to all this is a leadership which is responsible and accountable, and is forcefully committed to the welfare, growth and development of the whole country and all its people. Any other set of actions breeds exclusion, undermines legitimacy, destroys any hope of cohesion and throws out the consensus project.

When we look around the world, it is the abuse of power and its deadly effects that hit us in the face. It seems that politics has always been adversarial and will continue to be so. In such circumstances it would appear to be blind utopianism to write about consensus and cooperation as alternative guides to political action. This might be so. But as human beings who are capable of reason we cannot be content with the futilities of more of the same as the basis for policy-making. So the writer has a duty to persevere with the case for change. And the pulse begins to quicken when some Guyanese politicians in their manifesto for shared governance proclaim that:

> The new system of governance must facilitate national development, the enrichment of the nation and the involvement and security of all Guyanese by instituting appropriate provisions to address the political, economic and social concerns and aspirations of all groups. All significant political groups of society must be represented in the national executive decision-making process....[2]

While others declare that –

> It is critical that we engage one another in dialogue. We should always reach out and talk to each other. In this way, we would be fulfilling the mandate of all Guyanese as we share our differing views in the search for national consensus on the common objective of making this country a better place for all.[3]

With this quickening of the pulse comes the expectation that the immensely difficult task of translating philosophy into action is about to begin. Not in bilateral talks. These have failed too many times to give any hope of success but in serious and persevering *facilitated* efforts to solve the Guyanese dilemma. Appendix One gives a more detailed argument of facilitation as a way forward. It creates an environment in which debate and discussion come before negotiation and choice and we can understand and respect the fact that the other side also has right on its side. This can set in motion a train of events – including institutional design – out of which might grow respect and mutual trust and in time a people and a nation with a core set of values and common goals.

In Chapter Three, side by side with ideas for "Grand Coalition" government and a reformed "Westminster Model" I have put forward the very simple and less complicated notion of

Alternating Government. I have done this because I believe that one of the central conditions of democracy is that the party in opposition should have a realistic chance of forming a government after open and honest elections. If this is not possible because of built-in ethnic cleavages or fraud, then the democratic edifice collapses. The excluded begin to feel that they are no longer bound by decisions to which they have not consented. In such circumstances there will be continuing mayhem. I have therefore argued for a reconstructed "Westminster Model" where the opposition has a constitutional right to govern at regular prescribed intervals. This is not selfishness or greed. It is one of the crucial attributes of being human. Upon this satisfaction of that human need for periods of real control lies, in my view, the road to peace and development in Guyana. This is compounded several times over when slavery and indenture are part of the common cultural inheritance. Extended exclusion from periodic access to real power savours of a return to domination. It simply will not do.

Finally, it bears repeating that the central purpose of this book is to suggest pathways towards the evolution of a Guyanese people. That is, the growth in a divided multi-ethnic society of a minimum number of agreed values and goals which are dedicated to the common good. This minimum homogeneity, it is argued, comes out of engineered conditions for inclusion, cooperation across boundaries, and on projects which build trust and encourages the legitimacy which comes from an actively participating community of citizens[4]. These are also the hallmarks of need satisfaction, democratic politics in action and respect for diversity.

At a more general level, this book is about the quest for a better Guyana. It is about leaving behind the remnants of a damaging colonial inheritance and relentlessly pursuing the search for an alternative framework of ideas, institutional designs and enlightened practices with which to live our lives and which might make a deeply divided society work for all its members. It is therefore about enlightenment, transformation and reconstruction after colonialism and its culture have taken their leave. For domination did not serve us well and must share the burden of responsibility not only for our debacle but for some of the most enduring problems of our time.

This book seeks to understand where we want to go as a people and how we might travel in order to get there. It is the travelling which is important here. For if we are determined enough, our knowledge and understanding will grow as we confront and solve, collaboratively, the problems which will inevitably challenge us as we go along. For our problems might not always be amenable to our existing approaches and will demand all our critical abilities and creative imaginations to counter them. And these will bring in their wake changes, new approximations, new problems and who knows, shifting goals. It is the will to learn from our mistakes, to confront them with passion and intuition, not dogma or blind prejudice, which will matter.

This shifting frontier of knowledge and experience which expands as we solve our problems and encounter new ones is where the excitement and satisfaction of our approach to political life must lie. It is the way in which we will roll back the crippling effects of colonialism and generate, in concert, solutions which are authentically our own. The importance of this search for authenticity cannot be overestimated. It is what will liberate us, restore our pride and dignity as human beings, and allow us entry into a more satisfying life. The study therefore notes in passing how we got to where we are today and the damage which lingers on. This understanding might not rid us completely of our scars but the constant activity of problems – trial solutions – mistakes – error correction – might help us to construct a future based on peaceful coexistence and active cooperation.

The core assumption of this work is that while we cannot rule out the possibility of partition as a solution to our challenges, the children of Guyana still wish to live together in one state. Therefore, given the coincidence between ethnic cleavage, political loyalty and adversarial politics, the challenge is how to work with this division in order to create a minimum cohesion from which all can benefit. In addition to freedom, dignity and the rule of law, it is my view that a multi-ethnic society needs goals concerning security for all, mutual recognition of identities, full participation in things that matter and justice in the distribution of social goods. These are conditions for legitimacy. They are also the necessary conditions of democratic politics. They were not given attention during colonial rule. Here, rules were handed down to be obeyed, and debates and arguments – democratic prerequisites – had no effective place beyond the fence of the colonial elite. They created an environment which bred virtue into authoritarianism. It is not surprising therefore that liberal democratic values which surrounded independence stumbled at the first hurdle.

Somewhere in the tangled bowels of Guyana's transplanted ethnic mix, its colonial and neo-colonial culture of divide and rule, the use of stereotypes to foster suspicion, resentment and fear and the effect of all this on human relationships, lies a monumental problem to be unravelled and solved. This work attempts to make preliminary inroads into that predicament. It does this on the proposition that knowledge and understanding of our world progresses through the way we face problems and attempt to solve them. Refusal to do so in a serious and sustained way is to invite extinction. In other words it seeks to set out the outlines of a philosophy for thought, action and the management of change in complex and troubled postcolonial societies like Guyana. In this sense philosophy is about how we organise and live our lives for mutual satisfaction. It is not about high sounding academic discourses on the nature of politics, the state, power, or authority, nor is it about the works of the great philosophers even though acknowledged borrowings from the great works will take place. It is about examining the assumptions which underpin our views of our world and so it concerns us all. Although the focus is on Guyana, there is resonance for the global post colonial dilemmas of the twenty-first century.

END NOTES

1. Seecoomar, J. (2002), *Contributions Towards the Resolution of Conflict in Guyana,* Leeds, Peepal Tree Press, p 244.
2. PNC/R (Oct. 16, 2002), 'On Shared Governance.'
3. PPP/C (Feb.11, 2003), 'Towards Greater Inclusive Governance in Guyana.'
4. Chryssochoou, D.N. (2001), *Theorising European Integration*, London, Sage Publications, p. 182

APPENDIX 1

GUYANA – IDENTIFYING A WAY FORWARD – JUDAMAN SEECOOMAR

In order to identify a way forward for Guyana, I have to break into the development conundrum which proclaims that there can be "no development without peace; [and] no peace without development."[1] I am choosing to give primacy to politics and so focus on the first part of the proposition – peacemaking – because according to Edward Azar "peace is development in the broadest sense of the term.[2] In a careful analysis of conflict and its debilitating impact on Guyanese progress Professor Ralph Premdas argues that a prerequisite for economic development in multi-ethnic states is the establishment of "legitimate political authority through cross communal reconciliation and power sharing."[3]

A starting point for this breakout must be the public recognition by the people and their chosen representatives:

- That the conflict is ours and if we are going to continue to live side by side, we will have to make peace together. No one else can do it for us.
- That the only way in which this peacemaking can be done is through serious and sustained dialogue. Dialogue in which the alternative futures are examined openly, honestly, and rigorously, and choices made which will benefit all the people.
- That the alternative – violence – does not resolve problems. It only intensifies them.
- That peacemaking which seeks to deal with root causes is a monumental task and is rarely possible through the independent actions of the parties themselves. Expert

help exists in the international community and should
be tapped if breakout of the deadlock into which we have
worked ourselves is to take place.

It is at this point that the international community comes
into its own. And this is the first step on the way forward. It
is incumbent upon those who have moral, economic or political
leverage and who truly care, to use their good offices to encourage
the Guyanese political leadership to embrace the importance
of the foregoing four propositions and be willing to act upon
them.

The second step comes when the parties to the Guyanese
conflict decide to engage in earnest and far reaching efforts
to move on from the debilitations of stalemate. This is likely
to be a long, difficult and brittle process and requires a committed
and tenacious sponsor. One who is prepared to stay the course,
finance the process, provide back up, give unending moral support
and most important of all provide a facilitator or team of
facilitators to guide the process. And all this for humanitarian
convictions and without selfish interests.[4]

The British and Irish Prime Ministers and the American
President together with Senator George Mitchell and his
facilitating team are one example of sponsorship and facilitation
in action. Another is the Norwegian government and Terje
Larsen and his team in Oslo. Together, they provide the gold
standard for the modern nonviolent peacemaking process.[5]

Two sets of comments are necessary for important aspects
of facilitated dialogue as peacemaking. The first concerns the
role of facilitator and the second, the agenda for the process.

(1) The role of the facilitator (or team of facilitators).

Peacemaking by dialogue is a fragile and accident prone process.
The chances of success are increased by the introduction of a
skilled third party into the process from the beginning. He/
she/they would have no mandate to make judgements, apportion
blame, take sides, exert pressure, encourage compromise or

peddle solutions. Their role is one of supportive neutrality. They work to create the type of environment in which the parties to a protracted conflict can engage in analysis rather than the use of force. Because of the professionalism and knowledge they bring to the process, they are a reservoir of ideas and can provide additional insights into the problems which confront the parties.[6]

Theirs is a delicate task. They have to provide the conditions in which parties who have been pursuing acrimonious policies towards each other can convert their conflict into a shared problem. They can then begin to identify its important elements and to engage collaboratively in the search for acceptable solutions. Any negotiations, any compromises, must come from the parties themselves. This passage from acrimony to collaboration is one which facilitation must smooth and guide but not direct. It is a voyage of discovery which those in dialogue must undertake together but reach independently. It is this goal of mutual acceptability which increases the possibility that any outcome would be self-sustaining.[7]

Facilitators gain their initial credibility because of their standing in the world, their knowledge, experience, and skill particularly in the handling of conflict. They have to be able to orchestrate group interaction without being directive, establish rapport and better understanding between the parties and to promote effective deliberation in matters of substance. They have to establish a reputation for neutrality and have the ability to respect confidentiality. They have to be alert and sensitive to what is at stake for those involved in the struggle.[8]

All this talent and more is required to create conditions for analysis, mutual exploration of differing points of view, the generation of new ideas, the costing of options and the cooperative solving of problems.[9]

(2) The agenda for peacemaking.

In the end the peacemaking agenda is a decision for the parties to the conflict. As Senator George Mitchell reported, it can be a long, frustrating, and painful process.[10] In this section I want to argue that since it is the peoples' welfare which is at stake, their ideas for their future demands careful attention. Moreover success for any programme for change will need their wholehearted support and cooperation. Hence the need to take them on the journey.

In a series of interviews conducted in 1997 for another study[11] the people were asked to discourse upon:

(A) Why, in their view, had Guyana arrived at its present state of political development, and

(B) What might be done to transform it into a decent society.

The following were distilled from the conversations:

(1) More than 30 years on from colonialism and its culture of obedience and subjecthood no deliberate attempt has been made to encourage the growth of an independent citizenry, let alone the development of a Guyanese people. In fact, inept political leadership has encouraged the hardening of divisions based on race as a means of gaining and holding on to power.

(2) This political entrepreneurship has led to widespread insecurity, uncertainty and fear, and the paralysis which comes from viewing all Guyanese life through the prism of race.

(3) To breakout of this entrapment requires institutions and practices which expunge the idea of winning and losing from the Guyanese political vocabulary and the enshrining of sharing as a central tenet of our public philosophy.

(4) Institutions which sincerely share power and authority at the national and local levels might begin the movement towards responsible citizen behaviour and habits of functional cooperation in the name of the greater good. And maybe from this might emerge a recognisable sense of being Guyanese.

(5) Because a truly functioning democracy demands some homogeneity of purpose, and because this is not likely to happen spontaneously in a polarised polity, the

institutions and practices which are designed to encourage its development must meet the existential needs of all the people. These are, it is suggested, needs for security, participation, recognition, identity, and distributive justice which must be satisfied if social order is to be maintained.

The foregoing are extrapolations from the evidence. In their own words the Guyanese spoke of the need for a new generation of leaders who were honest and fair and who had the interest of the whole country as their constituency. Some spoke of governmental institutions which shared power and responsibility proportionately while others advocated national unity governments, federalism, or regionalism. Only one respondent seriously made the case for partition. Greater involvement of civil society was seen as crucial, as was an equal role for women. Participation and inclusion in decision-making were bywords, as were fairness in the allocation of land, jobs, and contracts. The importance of educational provision, the willingness to recognise that ethnic differences exist and should be dealt with frontally, the return of identifiable constituency representatives instead of the anonymity of lists associated with proportional representation, an independent judiciary and unbiased policing all featured in the Guyanese glimpses of their future and on their agenda for change.

If after a period of intense deliberation the Guyanese are able to agree on a programme for democratic advance, the international community has to stand on the sidelines, encouraging but not interfering and willing to help but only when asked. During this period of implementation it is for the people and their leaders to make the determined effort, to persevere in the face of difficulties and to change tack if confrontation with reality suggests that this needs to be done.

In fact deep-rooted conflict is never resolved in one giant leap. As Popper puts it "with each step forward, with every problem we solve, we not only discover new and unsolved problems, but we also discover that just when we believed that we were standing on firm and safe ground, all things are, in reality, insecure and unstable."[12] Because of this a culture of problem solving has to be built into the management of conflict and change "so that adjustments to institutions and policies can take place in a continuing way as systems evolve, as conditions change, and as experience and increased knowledge suggest."[13]

In this paper I have chosen to concentrate on peacemaking because, in my view, peace, "a working democracy instead of a voting democracy,"[14] and development, are bedfellows. In this *menage*, peace takes the lead. The burden of my argument is for a pre-emptive strike. A strike, not for death and devastation but in the name of dialogue, negotiation and consensus which are preconditions for a way forward in Guyana.

END NOTES

1. McDonald, G.M. (1998), 'Alternative Perspectives in Building Peace in Columbia and El Salvador', Unpublished PhD dissertation, University of Bradford, p. 80.
2. Azar, E.E., (1986), 'Protracted International Conflicts: Ten Propositions' in Burton, J. and Dukes, F. eds. (1990), *Conflict: Readings in Management and Resolution,* London, Macmillan, p. 155.
3. Premdas, R.R. (1995), *Ethnic Conflict And Development: The Case of Guyana,* Aldershot, Avebury, p.155.
4. Burton, J. W. (1987), *Resolving Deep-Rooted Conflict: A Handbook,* Lanham, MD., University of America Press. pp. 33-35.
5. Seecoomar, J. (2002), *Contributions Towards the Resolution of Conflict in Guyana,* Leeds, Peepal Tree Press, Chap. 8.
6. Burton, J. W. (1987), p.43.
7. De Reuck, A. (1984), 'The Logic of Conflict: Its Origins, Development and Resolution', in Banks, M. (ed.), Conflict *in World Society: A New Perspective in International Relations,* Brighton, Wheatsheaf Books Ltd.
8. Mitchell, C. and Banks, M. 1996), *Handbook of Conflict Resolution: The Analytical Problem-solving Approach,* London, Pinter, p.x.
9. Light, M. (1984), 'Problem-Solving Workshops: The Role of Scholarship in Conflict Resolution.' in Banks, M. ed. *Conflict in World Society: A New Perspective on International Relations,* Sussex, Wheatsheaf. pp. 15-34.
10. Mitchell, G, (1999), *Making Peace,* London, Heinemann, p. 126.
11. Seecoomar, J. (2002), see chapter 5 for a sample from 100 hours of recorded interviews.
12. Popper, K, (1992), *In Search Of A Better World,* London, Routledge, p. 65.
13. Burton, J. W. (1997), *Violence Explained,* Manchester, Manchester University Press, p.13.
14. Mitrany, D. (1966), *A Working Peace System,* Chicago, Quadrangle Books, p. 36.

APPENDIX TWO.

RACE, DEMOCRACY, AND POWER SHARING.
DR DAVID HINDS.

[Presented at the Walter Rodney Memorial Lecture 19 July 2001, Tower Hotel, Georgetown.]

Introduction

Some forces, in particular the WPA – both as a party and through some of its members who have functioned in the academic sphere such as CY Thomas, Walter Rodney, and Eusi Kwayana – have correctly argued that development in Guyana would be non-existent, or at best stifled, without a political solution. During the first two and a half decades of independence when the country, unfortunately descended to authoritarianism, the main focus of that political solution was the return to electoral democracy and the unlocking of the police state.

While attention was given to the underlying problem of race, in hindsight, perhaps not enough vigorous emphasis was placed on the potential impact of this democratization on the historical racial competition and vice versa. Again, the WPA may have been the most perceptive in this regard, as its proposal in 1979 for a Government of National Unity, did in part attempt to address the issue of racial security. My contention here is that while due attention was paid to the mobilization of racial solidarity and unity as a means of confronting authoritarian rule, enough attention was not given to the racial consequences inherent in democratization in a multiracial country.

There were several assumptions as the prospect of electoral democracy materialized. First, it was assumed that the Indian and African working class had developed a high degree of solidarity that would carry over into the post-authoritarian period. Second, it was thought that the PNC that presided over the authoritarian state would be seriously diminished with the return of electoral democracy. Third, it was assumed that the anti-dictatorial parties would transfer their institutional relationship into a broad-based government. Fourth, many thought that the WPA with its multiracial or nonracial credentials would have been a serious electoral contender, thus becoming a balancer in the system. Finally, and perhaps the most damaging, it was assumed that the demise of authoritarianism would translate automatically to democratization.

That these assumptions turned out to be miscalculations has been painfully evident since 1992. The demise of authoritarianism can lead to any of the following three developments: democratization (both in form and substance); increased authoritarianism; and uncertainty in spite of formal democracy. From all appearances the experience in Guyana since 1992 places it squarely in the third category. The unleashing of the people's energies leading to creativity and productivity that was expected with the dawning of a new era, have not materialized. Instead, a despair comparable to the dark days of authoritarian rule is abroad. While the democratic form of competitive elections has been maintained, these have not led to more substantive democratization such as social equality, universal participation in governance, and political equality. In fact, while elections have been competitive, they have not been free from fear and corruption.

The underlying factor in this development has been race or more particularly, racial competition arising from racial insecurity. With the return of "free" elections, there has been a massive, almost absolute, return to racial solidarity, which in the context of the competition for state power degenerates into racial animosity. And with no authoritarian hand to suppress this animosity or serve as a lightning rod for racial solidarity, we have witnessed almost a decade of political uncertainty and instability, which have brought the country to a virtual standstill. As the two major contenders for power battle each other for the ultimate political prize, the entire country becomes consumed either as racial adversaries, helpless onlookers, or frustrated peacemakers.

While this political battle is almost five decades old, it has ironically gained maximum momentum with the demise of authoritarian rule. Ironic because authoritarian rule was in part, a result of this very political/racial battle that peaked in the 1960s. The PNC regime was a product of Cold War machinations, but it was also a product of African-Guyanese fear of Indian domination. This fear was translated into a desire for African domination. Fear of being dominated, therefore led to a perpetuation of domination.

The consequence of this battle for power has been twofold – political and socio-economic. As mentioned before political instability has been the order of the day. The political institutions have been incapable of arresting the unrest that has been both a cause and effect of instability. None of the three branches of government individually or in concert with each other has been able to stem the tide. The prime reason for this lack of government ineffectiveness is that government itself is the problem. It is the struggle for control of the government that has been at the heart of the unrest. Further, a combination of the mode of governance, the means by which government is created, the nature of government in our postcolonial experience and the historical racial competition and mistrust that constitute the political crisis in the country.

When a political party, which is not a guerrilla movement makes good on its pledge to make the country ungovernable, it is not only the patriotism of the party that must be questioned, but most importantly it is the political culture and the political system that must be seriously questioned. The Government has struggled to stamp its authority, a situation that has hampered its ability to push through its programs and to maintain law and order. Our continued failure to examine the problem in these broad terms has certainly been to our peril.

The workability of political systems is based in part on popular confidence. And by popular confidence I mean confidence by the broad cross section of the society, which in a multiracial society such as Guyana, must mean multiracial confidence. No one with any honesty can bear witness that our government enjoys popular multiracial confidence. There is, therefore, a serious political crisis in the country that paralyses the political institutions. In other words, the already shaky institutions have collapsed under the weight of the political competition for power. There is a crisis of both legitimacy and penetration.

On the economic front, nothing gets done. Economic development has stalled as investment and productivity – scarce commodities in the best of times – have dried up. In the process the poverty accumulated from centuries of economic exploitation has assumed epidemic proportions. This is manifested in the overflowing unemployment, squalid social conditions and their attendant social ills. Such a development has served as the perfect breeding ground for the narcotics trade that is fast compromising the health and integrity of the populace.

This combined economic and political crisis has engendered a prolonged period of uncertainty that has transformed the country into a time bomb that frequently goes off at the slightest irritation. And when a country tethers on the brink of anarchy and disintegration, the temptation to use coercive means under the guise of law and order is real. Resort to such means in a situation of racial animosity can have two consequences: Increased racial hostility and the institution of a police state, the latter being the first step to full blown dictatorship. The thin line between legitimate protest and criminal activity is just the kind of breeding ground for the use of state force. In the circumstances the threat of a return to authoritarianism is a real one.

The Case For Power Sharing
The deep crisis described above with its seemingly intractable nature requires a concerted effort to arrest the situation in the short run with the ultimate goal of turning it around in the long run. Because the problem is so far reaching, repair work must also be far reaching. It is difficult to point to any single root cause, for as the problem unfolds cause and effect become indistinguishable. But in our circumstances, our racial problem

will have to be the culprit. The question is where to start this repair work? I believe the first step is to begin a search for a formula that simultaneously addresses the following ills: racial insecurity and competition, undemocratic rule, and the attendant political and economic instability. In this regard we feel power sharing, conceived not as an abstraction but as a natural outgrowth of our circumstances, is a safe place to start.

The History

Power Sharing as an alternative form of governance to the current Westminster model is not new to the Caribbean region, having first been proposed by Eusi Kwayana in 1961 as a solution to the emerging racial disharmony in Guyana, and by Sir Arthur Lewis in 1965 in his attempt to find a solution to similar ethnic problems in Africa. Later on both Dr Cheddi Jagan and Dr Walter Rodney advanced it as a solution to Guyana's racial and economic problems. Arend Lijphart has since argued that it is a necessary solution to the inherent instability in plural societies – societies segmented along racial, ethnic, religious, linguistic, and other cultural lines.

Power Sharing has been practised in varying forms or degrees in several countries with varied success. The clear cases are Belgium, The Netherlands, Malaysia, Switzerland, Cyprus, Lebanon and Austria. Recent additions to this list are South Africa, Northern Ireland and Fiji. Further, more than twenty other countries have practised some form of Power-Sharing. All of these countries can be described as plural societies divided along racial, ethnic, or linguistic lines.

Third, in relation to Guyana there have been several Power-Sharing proposals over the last four decades.

The first of these was the Joint-Premiership proposal put forward in 1961 by Eusi Kwayana on behalf of the African Society For Racial Equality (ASRE).

This proposal, which was rejected by both major parties, essentially called for executive Power-Sharing between the PNC and the PPP as a means of preventing the impending racial explosion and helping in the search for national unity. It is important to note here that Kwayana is most remembered for his partition call. However, his proposal was "Joint-Premiership with Partition as a last resort."

The next Power-Sharing proposal came in 1963 when a mission headed by a Professor W E Abraham visited Guyana and proposed Executive power sharing with both parties, the PPP and the PNC, sharing important Ministries. Under pressure from the PNC-UF-TUC alliance, Dr. Jagan agreed, but Mr. Burnham, sensing his growing position of strength, wriggled out of it. According to Dr. Jagan (1970), this idea for power sharing was mooted earlier by a United Nations Committee (Committee of Seventeen), but Mr. Burnham similarly found a way out of it.

This writer has not come across any rejection of this version from the PNC. As an aside, it is interesting to note that while a locally sponsored proposal was rejected, a similar overseas-sponsored one was embraced. In 1976 the PPP proposed a "National Patriotic Front" which called for power sharing between itself and the PNC and other patriotic forces of 1976 and the WPA's "Government Of National Unity and Reconstruction" in 1979. Both proposals advocated Power-Sharing but differed on composition and ideological orientation. Whereas the PPP's NPF included the PNC and listed socialist orientation as a prerequisite, the WPA's GNUR excluded the PNC but did not have any ideological litmus test.

The PNC rejected the PPP's proposal while the WPA supported it in principle. On the other hand, the PPP balked at the WPA's GNUR on the grounds that it gave too much representation to the right wing. The PNC initiated talks with the PPP in 1985 towards a National Government including the two parties.

This initiative fell apart with the death of Mr. Burnham. Finally, in 1990 the WPA proposed an interim National Government to preside over the country as it prepared for its first free and fair post-independence elections. The PNC, though in power, expressed mild interest in the proposal, but the PPP poured cold water on it.

The Rationale

There has developed in each Caribbean country a "political tribalism" that is based on party affiliation whereby the masses are organized into competing political camps. As Tim Hector (2000) observes, the evolution of the two-party system in the Caribbean is really reflective of the division of the working classes into two antagonistic factions; thus the emergence of pluralism based on political tribalism. Given the racial polarization of Guyana, this tribalism has taken on a racial outlook.

As we observed earlier, this political tribalism has had a negative effect on the country's developmental process as it has served to stifle consensus, stability, and nationhood – key components of economic progress and democratization. In this atmosphere of polarization, the very tenets of Westminster democracy, bequeathed to the region at independence, which were meant to be stabilizing influences, have instead served to deepen the polarization and stifle democratic evolution. In particular, the government-opposition and winner-take-all majoritarian principles have been utilized in the consolidation of a segmented or non-neutral state based on party paramountcy and exclusionary governance.

In effect, then, the Westminster model has failed to translate formal democracy into a more substantive democracy that embraces genuine political equality. Allied to political democratization is the question of economic democratization: who owns the production systems? After 35 years of independence the working people of this country do not have any stake in the ownership of productive enterprises. Capital accumulation, instead, is largely concentrated in the hands of foreign interests and a small local elite.

The case for power sharing in Guyana, then, is premised on the following factors:

(a) the need to create forms of governance aimed at arresting the growing political instability and threat of social disintegration;
(b) the encouragement by the Westminster model of an

adversarial political culture and its concomitant failure
to guarantee consensus and shared nationhood;

(c) the need to arrest the slide towards another wave of
authoritarianism;

(d) allied to (c) is the need to transform the formal democracy
that currently exists into a substantive democracy based
on peoples power, political and racial equality, equality
of opportunity both socially and racially, and shared
nationhood; and

(e) the need to develop political arrangements consistent with
the emerging economic owning patterns.

This call for power sharing springs from the very concrete
situation in our country. As Kwayana (2001) points out in relation
to his 1961 proposal, "It was a solution, so far as I was concerned,
posed by the social and political logic of the situation then
before us and not by me."

Adversarial Politics
As a result of the political segmentation alluded to above, the
faction that gains control of government and state, often with
a slim majority, has generally governed in an authoritarian manner
that has led to the relegation of the minority faction to the
periphery of the political process. The fact that the minority
faction is usually only marginally smaller than the majority
faction has meant that almost half of the population is banished
from governance. This situation has served to intensify the
divisions in the society and has had a debilitating effect on
political and economic development. Kwayana observed the
genesis of this segmentation in 1961:

It was very clear to us in 1961 that 'Indians will not accept an
African ruler and Africans would not accept an Indian ruler...
The split in the national movement, and the idea of 'one leader'
meant that each of the two major parties, based in different races,
began to develop its own 'pre-nation' institutions... All of us,
came to regard Joint-Premiership, as a means of recombining two
separate pre nations back into one stream with the just aspirations
of each satisfied, but only the just aspirations, as each side had
other dreams too.

Governance in Guyana has, therefore, evolved into an exercise in political witch-hunting, party domination, marginalization of the losing faction, plunder of state resources as a means of personal enrichment and maintenance of state clientelism. And opposition has meant destabilization of the government. This brand of adversarial politics is inconsistent with Westminster culture, which puts national unity above partisan considerations. A key point here is that whereas in Westminster terms, opposition means "government in waiting", in the Caribbean's "Adapted Westminster", it is translated into marginalization of half of the populace, possibly permanently.

Tim Hector's observations of adversarial politics in Antigua are symptomatic of the situation in Guyana:

> The contention between the parties has produced since 1976 this heavy reliance on State patronage, which has distorted both politics and the economy… Adversarial politics is the competition between parties, not based on ideas of policy and program, but based on "I appoint and I disappoint", in opposition, but more so in government… Adversarial politics has reached the absurdity where politicians in power use every means to deny their opponents work for years; the right to practice their profession, and even to destroy by terrorist arson their means of livelihood. There is no longer, in appearance or in substance, Parliamentary democracy here, but an idea-less struggle for naked power, to appoint and disappoint by State patronage.

Here in Guyana there has developed a culture where domination is seen as the best defence against bullying by the opposite race group and then becomes an end in itself. This is a critical aspect of the intra-group convergence of expectations. It is shared and promoted by the respective leaderships of the two parties, thus cementing a political culture that is resentful of co-operation, consensus, and notions of equivalence and of united governance.

Critique of the Westminster Model in Plural Societies
In this regard the Westminster model in its present form, while effective in maintaining formal democracy, has proved to be a barrier to deepening that democracy and realizing national

consensus. A crucial deficiency in the Caribbean's experience with the Westminster model has been its inability to develop a Westminster culture, which is vital to the viability of the Westminster model.

Hence elections in Guyana are a high intensive exercise as the stakes are high – which race or political-tribal faction will gain the majority that guarantees total power? According to Sir Arthur Lewis (1965), democracy has two meanings: "The primary meaning is that all who are affected by a decision should have the chance to participate in making that decision, either directly or through representatives. Its secondary meaning is that the will of the majority will prevail." (p. 64) These two meanings, he contends, are mutually exclusive; it's either one or the other. The European countries chose the second meaning and imposed it on its colonies at independence. But Lewis insists that "to exclude the losing groups from participating in the decision-making clearly violates the primary meaning of democracy" (p.65) While the latter approach has worked relatively well in European societies, it has been far less effective in the plural societies of the ex-colonies.

This majoritarian principle in the Westminster culture assumes that the majority once in power will embrace and address those minority interests. Most European countries and the USA can claim success with this principle precisely because they are largely homogenous societies, which exhibit a considerable degree of consensus even when there is a disagreement on specific approaches.

The political culture, therefore, feeds off this consensus, thus making politics and the competition for political office a relatively low intensive exercise. Lewis concurs with this view when he likens elections under the Westminster model to "competition between businessmen to serve the consumer," and the emphasis is on " the politicians rather that the groups they represent" (p.65) and, therefore, as in business, if you win and take all, and if you lose, you lose everything. He however noted that in social institutions – family, church, university, and sports – Europeans stress compromise and teamwork rather than majority vote.

The term plural societies refers to those societies that are segmented along racial, linguistic, ethnic and other cultural lines.

Arend Lijphart, outlines four criteria for determining whether a society is plural:

1. Can the various segments into which the society is divided be clearly defined?
2. Can the size of each segment be exactly determined?
3. Do the segmental boundaries and the boundaries between the different political, social, and economic organisations coincide?
4. Do the segmental parties receive the stable electoral support of their respective segments?

If we accept this framework, and then it is clear that Guyana is one of the most plural societies, for it satisfies all four criteria. Even more, the segmental differences in Guyana have manifested themselves in violent confrontations from as early as the immediate post- emancipation era, culminating with the racial disorders of the 1960s.

But in plural societies, such as Guyana, because politicians represent distinct groups of people with differing communal and political-tribal interests, elections are translated into contests between these groups. Further, unlike the leaders in Europe and the USA, Guyanese leaders are less dispassionate about wining or losing elections since given the undeveloped nature of the society few prestigious options exist outside the political sphere. The situation is compounded by the fact that whereas in the "class-based societies" of Europe and North America group differences are based primarily on matters of ideology or socio-economic interests, in plural societies these differences result primarily from the fact that these groups are what Lewis calls "historical enemies" (p.66).

The consequence of this high intensive exercise was manifested in the last three elections in Guyana. While electoral malpractice was cited as the reason for the post election protests subsequent developments have shown that the underlying problem is the racial consequences of the winner-take-all system that threatens to institutionalize racial domination under the rubric of democracy. This has led to a crisis of governance that has compromised the governments' legitimacy, and to racial and political upheaval.

Professor Clive Thomas labels this development a "democratic contradiction" and sounded an ominous warning:

> Democracy confined to free and fair elections and ignoring ethnic security, and the needs and fears of the major race groups would not be sustainable… If racial voting were to be the outcome of a free and fair election next time around, then free and fair elections might well come to be seen as a pillar of domination rather than a democratic advance, thereby leading to its rejection, and increasing the prospects of social breakdown (p.26)

Beyond Westminster
It is against this background that the increasing calls for either a modification or abolishment of the Westminster model, in particular the elimination of the winner-take-all and government-opposition principles, and the institution of Power Sharing in the form of National Governments must be seen. It is part of the search for a way out of this crisis that is eating away at the very existence of our already fragile nation.

The case for Power-Sharing in Guyana assumes the following:

(1) that the various race groups, especially Africans and Indians, want to stay together as a nation; and
(2) that the guiding principles of the nation are peaceful coexistence, cooperation and mutual respect.

No group in a plural society voluntarily accepts the leadership of another group. The situation is compounded when that minority is a large one, as is the case in Guyana and Trinidad and Tobago. Unless a formula can be found to include these groups in the decision making process, nationhood will always be an elusive dream. And if there is no collective sense of nationhood, there can be no political stability and economic development. Guyana is a compelling witness to that truth.

As Lewis points out, "the democratic problem in a plural society is to create political institutions which give all the various groups the opportunity to participate in decision-making, since only then can they feel that they are full members of a nation, respected by their numerous brethren and giving equal respect to the natural bond which holds them together." (p.66)

Selwyn Ryan (1993:149) advocates some form of power sharing in Trinidad and Tobago and Guyana "where no one group wins everything or loses everything in the process" Clarence Ellis argues for power sharing as "the best mechanism for achieving inclusiveness in our racially divided and increasingly unstable society." Kwayana urges that Power Sharing "offers domination to neither leader, neither people, nor race, only human equality, not even equality of numbers." Tim Hector feels that power sharing would lead among other things to more government accountability:

> Only a government of national unity can, in the present economic and historical context raise the productivity of labour, and therefore national wealth. A Government of National Unity ensures the return of accountability, therefore a widening of the tax base, automatically becomes possible. This guarantees that with the inclusion of the opposition, people can have justifiable faith that their tax dollars will be spent as determined by their elected representatives with full accountability for every tax dollar. This process, and this process alone, probity in government, will unlock the mysteries of the spirit of progress and development

Elements of Power Sharing
According to Arend Lijphart, a definition of Power-Sharing or Consociational democracy includes the following elements:

(1) Government by a "grand coalition " of political parties and leaders representing the significant segments of a plural society. Such a "grand coalition" can take the form of a grand coalition cabinet and/or a coalition of top office holders such as a Multi-Person presidency or Prime-Ministership.

(2) Mutual veto by the different segments.

(3) Proportional representation as the method of arriving

at political representation, top civil service appointments
and allocation of public funds for economic development.
(4) Autonomy for the different segments to run their internal
affairs.

There are a few points to be noted here. First, Power Sharing
is likely to be most effective if it is constitutionally mandated.
In this regard Executive Power-Sharing is not a simple coalition
or marriage of convenience. As is pointed out above, it is a
"grand coalition" cabinet comprising the representative parties
and Cabinet positions are divided in proportion to the percentage
of votes acquired at election. What differentiates Power Sharing
from the simple coalition is that the former is constitutionally
mandated while the latter is not.

Second, any grand coalition must be premised on an agreed
national direction that includes agreement on a broad national
developmental program. Given the limited choices at the disposal
of small countries like Guyana, this is not a very difficult task.
Third, the leaders of the various segments must have a deep
and abiding commitment to the unity of the nation and must
be prepared to uphold the laws and the democratic process.
Cooperation and compromise must be the guiding principles
and must be predicated on a willingness of the leaders of one
segment to work with the other segments.

But even as the leaders try to cooperate with each other,
they must hold their respective constituencies together. In this
regard, the leaders must be more tolerant than their followers
and must have the ability to strike compromises in the interest
of the nation even when those compromises are not popular
with their 'followers'. These leaders must, according to Lijphart
"perform a difficult balancing act." Leaders must therefore be
bold, creative, and above all must have the trust of their followers.
Lijphart also makes the point that while it important for leaders
to carry the masses along, it is doubly important for them to
get the support of the second level leadership of the parties.
Another category that the leaders must consider when making
decisions is the non-political groups such as religious associations
and "ethnic" organizations.

Next to leadership, the size of the various segments is most crucial to Power-Sharing. In particular, the presence of a majority segment is seen as being unfavourable since the majority segment always has an eye on maintaining or reverting to Winner-Take-All. On the other hand, in cases where the two segments are of approximately equal size, the leaders tend to be more disposed to dialogue and negotiations. The fact that one side cannot easily overrun the other is enough reason for compromise.

Guyana does have a majority segment – Indians make up about 51% of the population with Africans making up about 44% according to the last census. The mixed races for the most part identify with themselves with the African Segment. Because the Indian segment is a bare majority that is not considerably larger than the African segment, there is somewhat of a balance. While the PPP has used the Indian majority to argue for Majoritarian Democracy, given the almost equal size of the African segment, it has found it difficult to govern in both of its stints in office. Further, the fact that the African segment dominates the military, and police apparatus and the civil service, it is able to wield considerable power outside the government.

Almost all the countries where Power-Sharing has been successful, the populations are relatively small. The advantage of small population size is that there is not an elaborate decision-making process and the leaders tend to know each other on a one-on basis. Of course small populations have their disadvantages – there is limited economies of scale and the pool of talent is smaller. However, for the purpose of consensus a small population is advantageous. Guyana has a population of approximately three-quarters of a million. Its leaders know each other personally and the decision making process is quite straightforward.

The grand coalition formula has been used by Western homogeneous societies during times of emergencies such as war. Most western countries experience a show of unity by the political parties. In instances such as during World War II, Britain actually formed a Grand Coalition Government or National Government. While the crisis in these societies tends to be temporary, thus needing temporary arrangements, the crisis in plural societies is permanent or as Lijphart says "It is the nature of the society that constitutes the crisis."

Since the "single dominant" leader characterises the Presidential system of government, it is in principle incompatible with Consensus democracy. However, it could be used with some alteration. One variation is the "joint presidency" or multi-person presidency where the various segments are represented with each having a veto over the other. An example of this arrangement is the seven-member Swiss Federal Council that is representative of the electoral strength of the four major parties, the different cantons, and the regions.

Another variation is the alternating presidency whereby the parties/segments rotate the presidency by either terms or the individual terms are split, which Lijphart calls diachronic "grand coalition". This arrangement works best in situations where there are two major segments such as in Guyana. Although Colombia is not a consensus democracy, it used this arrangement for the period 1958-74. In the Swiss Federal Council the presidency is rotated annually among the members. Yet another variation is the Lebanese Model of linking the presidency with the executive positions such as the Prime Minister, Vice President and Deputy Prime Minister in a kind of ruling coalition.

A key element of Consensus Democracy is Separation of Powers, especially between the executive and the legislative. Such clear separation ensures that each branch serves as a check on the other. It also allows the legislative branch to function as a kind of opposition to the executive branch and mediator among the segments. Where there are deadlocks in the cabinet, these matters could be referred to the legislature for resolution. For such a system to work best cabinet members cannot be members of the legislature.

Success and Failure
Some critics have argued that because consensus democracy has declined in countries such as Austria and Holland, it has failed. But in fact, this decline is a reflection of the success of the model in minimizing the divisions in those societies. By the same token the breakdown of Power-Sharing in Lebanon

was not the result of its failure but the result of external pressure on the country. Power Sharing lasted for 32 years in Lebanon 1943 -1995, during which time the four main religious segments – Christian, Sunni Muslim, Shiite Muslim and Greek Orthodox shared the governance of the country. Despite several instances of conflict, including a civil war in 1958, the system survived.

In the case of the South Africa, the parties agreed beforehand that it was going to be an interim government. Clearly the presence of the grand coalition played a pivotal role in halting the violence and facilitating a smooth transition from apartheid.

Another successful case of Power-Sharing was in Malaysia 1955-1969. This arrangement broke down when the three main parties that formed the Grand Coalition lost a sizable portion of their popular support to other parties in the 1969 elections. One may argue that this was a good development except that these other parties were communal parties, which influenced the civil disorder.

One of the problems with Malaysia was that despite the Power-Sharing arrangement most of the national symbols were reflective of the Malay segment, which comprised 53% of the population. This, in addition to the electoral system – single member district – gave a disproportionate representation of the Malays in the Grand Coalition. These two factors no doubt eliminated the other segments and influenced the eventual breakdown of the system. Had the system been reviewed and adjusted to meet the changes in the society, the civil disorder may have been prevented.

The one real failure of Consensus Democracy was in Cyprus 1960. Despite having the perfect consensus constitution, the country erupted in civil war after only a few years. The major reason for this breakdown was the fact that there was a very large majority Greek segment (78%).

The Turks comprised a mere 18%. But the Turks were awarded the Vice-Presidency, three out of ten cabinet seats and five out of 50 parliamentary seats! The same ratio applied to the Civil Service while there was a 6:4 ratio for the police and army. In addition the Vice President had equal powers to the Greek President and an equal veto over the cabinet and legislature on matters of defence, security and Foreign Affairs. The Turks therefore were over represented and tended to stick to the letter of the constitution. The Greeks on the other hand had reluctantly accepted the constitution at the time of Independence and their attempt to alter the constitution to achieve stricter proportionality sparked the civil war that led to the breakdown of Power-Sharing. But apart from the internal dynamics, the situation was influenced by the fact that both Greece and Turkey intervened on the sides of their respective nationals.

Answering the Critics

Now, to some of the arguments that have been raised about the weaknesses or unworkability of Power Sharing.

Gridlock

Gridlock is inherent in any system of governance. While situations of crisis and emergency demand prompt decision-making, hastily executed decision-making is contrary to democratic governance as it downplays democratic tenets such as consultation, extensive deliberations, compromise and consensus. Even the Westminster Model which is the least gridlocked of the political systems has certain built-in delay mechanisms such as the House of Lords' suspensory veto whereby that body can hold up passage of a bill for up to six months. True, an all-party cabinet moves gridlock into the executive branch, but the same gridlock exists in single party executives where various factions of the party invariably battle over policy.

Gridlock has the potential of frustrating decision-making but the threat of gridlock also forces compromise, if not consensus. It expands the scope for broad discussion and deliberation that make for more broad-based decisions.

This is most crucial for seriously divided societies such as Guyana as such an exercise does two important things –

(a) it institutionalizes a culture of working together and

(b) it produces decisions that have the support of the various factions. Finally extreme gridlock occurs in any system from time to time over fundamental issues. This is good for democracy for decisions on fundamental issues must by democratic necessity invite inputs from as wide a cross section of society as possible. If cabinet fails to settle an issue, then the parliament must be empowered to settle it.

In the case of Guyana one must note that we have been gridlocked for almost six decades, in particular since 1997. The government has been unable to get much done as the opposition has used its street power and support within the state apparatus to frustrate decision-making.

The current confusion between government action and the work of the dialogue committees is a case in point. Had the PPP and the PNC been in the cabinet together, there would have been less confusion and time consumption.

Institutionalization of Racial Voting Patterns
Again the charge ignores the Guyanese reality. Racial voting patterns have been institutionalized for a long time now and can hardly be further institutionalized. Any corrective measure must start with that admission and must in the first instance move to create conditions to prevent this racial voting pattern from giving rise to racial violence, discrimination and domination. Whether power sharing will solve our racial problems and/or change racial voting is speculative, but what is certain is its ability to neutralize the consequences of racial voting by forcing the contending forces to work together for the common good. It would be more correct to say that power sharing will not immediately get rid of racial voting. But it does encourage the less hard-core racial voters to vote for a third force, as such a vote would not be seen as a "wasted vote", given the fact that the intensity of the competition for racial control of the government will be lowered considerably.

The creation of this third force will be crucial as it will serve as a balancer in the system; thus reducing the threat of extreme gridlock.

Abolishing of Opposition
This is perhaps the most glaring benefit of Power Sharing for Guyana. Government in Guyana has meant government by one race and opposition has meant opposition by the other

race. This equation has served to create instability and erase the other races, especially the Amerindians, from the political mix. Opposition has really been an exercise in destabilization of the government; the opposition has functioned more as a parallel government than a government in waiting.

Under power sharing, the place for opposition is the legislative branch, which has to be translated into a real oversight of the executive branch. In this regard there has to be more separation of powers then currently obtains whereby a minimum of ministers sit in parliament. This would allow for a fresh set of eyes and minds to look at bills when they reach the parliament.

Dividing Office among Elites

What's new? We operate under a representative form of democracy which given the size of the population, is much more manageable than direct democracy.

People elect their representatives who do not generally reflect their class interests given our history of elite domination of political parties. However, in Guyana's case, these elites represent the racial desires of their followers to control governmental power. Elite control of power is a given in Guyana. But a "vertical power sharing" or devolution of power to the local governments can counterbalance this. In this regard, the return to village government is key to power sharing. This allows for both racial and class empowerment – racial because of the racial homogeneity of our villages and class because more working class people are likely to be elected to village councils.

Power Sharing is not anti-Westminster

Power Sharing is not anti-Westminster in principle. It really is a modification of Westminster as it seeks to tailor the model to the peculiarities of segmented societies. The casualties here are the majoritarian and winner-take-all principles – principles that presuppose a political culture that is not part of our heritage. But other aspects of Westminster such as parliamentary or legislative supremacy are retained. In fact our current system has strayed from the principle of legislative supremacy, where the parliament hires and fires the executive.

Our system is a Presidential-Parliamentary system based on executive supremacy along the lines of the French system. The President and cabinet are not answerable to Parliament in any institutionalized manner. What we have is "legislative pretence," where the executive basically controls the process with little or no check by the legislature. A crucial example of this is the fact that there can be no legislative vote of confidence in the executive.

Some Concrete Proposals
The Power Sharing Government shall be based on the following principles:
- Proportional Representation
- Separation of Powers
- Checks and Balances
- Central Government

The Executive Branch:
The Executive branch shall comprise a two or three person Executive Presidency and a Cabinet.

The Presidency:
There shall be a three-person Executive Presidency including the representative of the parties with the three highest numbers of votes at the election.

The party with the highest number of votes shall hold the Presidency, and the one with the second highest shall hold the Prime Ministership and Vice Presidency and the one with the third highest will hold the Deputy Prime Ministership and Second Vice Presidency.

The latter must garner at least 10% of the vote to be included in the presidency. If no single third party gets that number of votes, but a coalition of parties does, then they shall choose some one to represent them. If the minor parties together do not meet the 10 percent threshold, there shall be a two-person presidency There shall be no special elections for these offices, each official shall have a veto, and belong to the cabinet.

Powers of the President
Commander in chief of the armed forces and Minister of Defence
    Perform the ceremonial functions of the Head of State.
    Represent the country at international functions.

Powers of the Prime Minister
Chairperson of the Cabinet
    Leader of Government Business in the House (but with no
voting powers)
    Minister of Home Affairs and National Security
Powers of Deputy Prime Minister
Chair of the House of Civil Society
    Vice-Chair of Cabinet
    Minister of Economic Planning and Development

Joint Powers
1. Approve or veto bills passed by Parliament
2. Nominate magistrates and judges, Police Commissioner,
   Head of the armed forces and the top governmental officials.
3. Appoint and fire Cabinet Members
4. Report to the Parliament on the State of the Nation twice
   per year.
5. Decide on the size of the cabinet, but it shall not exceed
   20 members.

Cabinet
Cabinet shall be a coalition of all parties that qualify for seats
in the parliament and shall be proportionally allocated. No
party shall hold more than three of the following ministries:
Finance, Economic Planning Development, Home Affairs and
National Security, Foreign Affairs, Education and Health.

    Cabinet decisions shall be based on consensus, but should
there be a vote, decisions must have the support of two-thirds
of the cabinet. Should Cabinet be unable to make a decision,
the matter shall be returned to parliament for resolution. Members
of the Cabinet may sit in the National Assembly and introduce
government bills, but they cannot vote.

Legislature

There shall be a bicameral legislature including an elected People's House of Representatives and an appointed Chamber of Civil Society. Election to the PHR shall be based on a mixed system of Proportional Representation and First Past the Post (FPTP) system.

The Peoples House of Representative shall comprise elected members, and non-voting members of the Cabinet and the Regional Councils.

Powers

Remove any member of the Executive Branch, including Cabinet Ministers, through a vote of no confidence, which must be initiated by at least one-third of the Lower House and passed by a three-quarters majority.

Override executive vetoes with a three-quarters vote.

Pass bills that relate to all areas of life in the country.

Settle any unresolved disagreements within the Executive Branch with a three-fifths vote.

Elect a speaker with a three-fifths vote.

Approve Executive nominations for the Judicial Branch and other top appointments.

Chamber of Civil Society

The Chamber of Civil Society shall comprise representatives of Civil Society Organizations including the TUC, Women's organizations, Guyana Bar Association, Guyana Council of Churches, The Private Sector Commission, and Youth Organization.

Review and endorse bills passed by the People's House of Representatives.

Hold a bill for up to three months pending review by the House of Representatives.

Local Government

The primary local government unit shall be the Village and Town Councils whose elections shall be based on a mixed electoral system.

Powers

The Power to tax.

Dual control with the Central Government over Education, Sanitation, and Public Works including drainage and irrigation and road repairs.

Regional Councils

Comprising representatives of Village and Town Councils. Representatives shall sit as non-voting members of the House of Representatives.

Powers

Oversight of Village Councils.

Approve budget of Councils.

Link between the Village and Town Councils and the Central Government.

APPENDIX 3

PNC/R ON SHARED GOVERNANCE

I. SHARED GOVERNANCE

Background

1. In recent months there has been much discussion on the issue of shared governance. The public debate has been given considerable impetus as a result of the Leader's Address to the party's congress. The statement that "adjusted governance is an idea whose time has come" has made it necessary for the party to develop firm positions on the principles of the new governance arrangements.

II. PRINCIPLES UNDERPINNING SHARED GOVERNANCE

2. The new system of governance must facilitate national development, the enrichment of the nation and the involvement and security of all Guyanese by instituting appropriate provisions to address the political, economic and social concerns and aspirations of all groups.

3. All significant political groups of society must be represented in the national executive decision-making process. Proportional representation (as determined by periodic national election) should be used to fix each party's level of involvement in the national government.

4. Measures must be put in place to enable appropriate representation of special groups (e.g., women, Amerindians, youths) in the national decision-making process.

5. Predetermined structures and procedures must be enshrined in the constitution or in any multiparty agreement to facilitate decision-making by consensus and to resolve disputes in the national executive.

6. The larger the margin of victory of the winning party, the fewer should be the inhibitions to the exercise of its powers in the multi-party executive.

7. The executive and legislative decision-making processes must be designed to discourage foot-dragging and undue delays by setting decision deadlines beyond which special mechanisms would be triggered.

8. The parliamentary committee on constitution reform must keep the new political arrangement under constant review through its own research and analysis, and by encouraging and examining submissions from the public.

9. The inclusionary democracy approach should infuse all aspects of national decision-making that have to do with resource allocation (tender boards, state boards, land selection committees, etc.).

10. The new government must be subject to independent, powerful and effective mechanisms of oversight and scrutiny.

11. The new system of governance must mandate the participation of the public and civic society in national decision-making.

12. The new system must expressly provide mechanisms for the economic empowerment of the disadvantaged.

13. There must be broad agreement on a national developmental programme.

III. FACILITATIVE CONDITIONS FOR SHARED GOVERNANCE IN GUYANA

14. Several conditions promote the potential for success of multiparty governance in Guyana:

- The ability of the major parties to sit and discuss rationally (the Constitutional review process),
- the presence of strong partiocracy (the situation when parties can control or manage the actions of their supporters, thereby maximising the chances that agreements struck among party leaders will be respected by most party members). This factor is advanced as one of the main reasons for the success of Belgian's power sharing government,
- the interests of international stakeholders (financial institutions) in preventing failure, "convergence" of ideologies among the main parties (a point in case: both major parties have publicly endorsed free enterprise).

IV. NON-EXECUTIVE HEAD OF STATE

15. The committee recommends the establishment of a non-executive President as Head of State. The presidency will constitute a moral, symbolic and, in a few cases, statutory authority standing over and above the dynamics of party politics. The nature and extent of the statutory authority is to be agreed on.

16. Specific functions will include:

- Assenting to bills,
- Acting as Commander-in-chief of the arm forces (see para. 54),
- Acting as a mediator in unresolved political disputes (see para. 36-37),
- Appointing presidential commissions of inquiry into suspected government misconduct.

17. Appointment. The president will be appointed for a seven-

year renewable term on a multi-party vote in parliament. A seven-year term ensures the presidency straddles the holding of national elections and reduces the pressure on the office-holder to pander to the parties in hopes of reappointment.

18. Removal. During his/her term of office, the president could be removed only on specified grounds by a weighted parliamentary vote.

V. EXECUTIVE DECISION-MAKING STRUCTURE AND PROCEDURES IN THE MULTI-PARTY GOVERNMENT

19. The make-or-break point in shared-governance arrangements is the decision-making process in the multiparty executive. Based on research of coalition (power sharing) governments of several countries (New Zealand, Finland, Sweden, Netherlands, Iceland, Belgium, and Ireland), the committee considers the following ideas best suited to Guyana's conditions.

20. Adopting the practice of most coalition governments, the partners in the government must first work out and sign a Coalition Agreement. The agreement must encompass:

- a policy platform (based on the national development program and a merger of ideas from party manifestoes),
- portfolio allocation and party responsibilities, and
- the decision-making structures and procedures within the executive.

21. The agreement must be publicised, as the public then can monitor the process and assess the compliance of coalition partners with the spirit and provisions of the agreement and the constitution.

22. The primary objective of the coalition decision-making process must be to facilitate consensus and to avoid surprises (significant unannounced unilateral action) by setting up rigid mechanisms for communication, consultation and dispute resolution within the executive itself.

23. Decision-making in the governing executive will be a mixture of collective responsibility (where consensus has been reached) and single-party responsibility (where no consensus has been reached or where unilateral actions are allowed).

Council of Ministers (Cabinet)

24. The Council of Ministers will be the highest executive decision-making body. It will comprise all ministers of government, parliamentary secretaries and (probably) government advisors. The Council is the point through which all cabinet matters must be channelled for discussion and approval. These matters are:

- all policy issues,
- proposals that will affect government's financial position or commitments,
- matters concerning the machinery of government,
- decisions and actions, allowed under the statutory powers granted to Ministers, that would affect the collective interest of government,
- proposals involving new legislation or regulations,
- government responses to select committee recommendations,
- controversial matters,
- all but the most minor public appointments,
- the release of important government documents, papers and reports,
- matters affecting the interests of a number of ministries.

25. The Council will be chaired by the Prime Minister and will meet at stipulated times. A quorum will be two-thirds of the members of each of the major parties.

26. Decisions will be by consensus, failing which the matter is sent for resolution to the Standing Coalition Management Committee.

Standing Coalition Management Committee

27. The Coalition Management Committee comprises the leaders (and possibly also senior party members) of the political parties in the Council. It is therefore a forum of summiteers (similar to the current inter-party dialogue), with two important roles: overall management of the coalition arrangement and to serve as the highest forum for dispute resolution.

28. The management committee will meet as often as necessary, and could be summoned at the request of any party leader in the coalition. The Prime minister will chair meetings. To form a quorum, all the major parties must be represented.

Ministerial Working Groups

29. The main arenas for consultation, coordination and negotiation among parties will be the standing Ministerial Working Groups. These are sub-committees of the Council of Ministers, comprising, at minimum, key ministers from the coalition groups, selected MPs, civil service heads and government advisers. Mandates of sub-committees should be broad enough to facilitate coordination among related government ministries. Suggested fields include foreign affairs, economic policy, and social policy.

30. From the experience of other countries, working groups are most effective as informal decision-making forums (referred to in Finland as "government evening classes"). Their fundamental objective is to process issues so that they need only be formally dealt with at full meetings of the Council of Ministers.

31. All initiatives (whether bills, policies, etc) from the various Ministries therefore must be first sent to the relevant subcommittee, as the first point of inter-party discussion and bargaining, before being forwarded to the Council of Ministers.

32. Notwithstanding, the Council may delegate authority to a subcommittee to make final decisions.

Procedures for Unresolved Issues

33. Preparations have to be made for those occasions when internal mechanisms for achieving consensus fail. These so-called "agree to disagree" situations, hopefully, should be rare, but have to be managed to avoid destabilising the coalition.

34. The basic requirement is for unresolved issues to be in relation to different party positions, and not in relation to difference in opinions of individual Ministers. In fact, dissociation of individual Ministers from Council decisions outside the agreed coalition processes should be discouraged.

35. Unresolved issues are treated differently depending in which of the two categories they fall:

- those a coalition party identifies as inimical to race relations in the country, and
- those that are identified as issues of "party distinction".

Matters harmful to race relations

36. Any initiative put forward by a party in the coalition that any of its major partners declares to be potentially harmful to race relations can pass only on a vote of a majority of members of each party in the Council or in the parliament (in Belgium, a party can exercise a suspensive veto to temporary stop the measure). If all attempts at internal dispute resolution fail, the matter is sent to the State President for a judgement. However, he/she must first seek advice, and any guidelines for correction, from the Ethnic Relations Commission, which must hold a public hearing on the matter.

37. If the Head of State, acting in accordance with the ERC, rules that the measure is indeed harmful to race relations, the

coalition partner must withdraw and amend the measure along the proposed guidelines before resubmitting it to the Ministerial working group. If the Head of State rules that the measure is not harmful to race relations, the matter could be implemented and is considered a collective decision of the Council.

Matters of "Party Distinction"

38. Unresolved matters identified by a coalition partner, other than the proposing party, as an issue that fundamentally separates the parties are sent to the parliament. There, the appropriate parliamentary sectoral committee must discuss the matter in a public session, before submitting its recommendations to the full House. Parties are allowed in speech and in vote to differentiate on the issue. The matter requires a simple majority to pass, and dissenting parties are no longer under any obligation of collective responsibility for that particular issue.

VI. ALLOCATION OF MINISTERIAL PORTFOLIOS

39. The number of portfolios each qualified party is entitled to will be determined by the election results. Parties have to garner above a minimum threshold of votes (5%) to qualify to join the governing coalition.

40. The Prime Ministership goes to the party that garnered the largest national support.

41. Distribution of portfolios will be as follows:

- The number of Ministries and their responsibilities would be fixed by Acts of Parliament.
- Stage 1: the parties attempt to decide on allocation through discussion within a specified timeframe (a week?).
- Stage 2: if no agreement is reached in the first stage, the selection process is done by an alternating pick system based on the principle of largest remainder, with the party with the largest number of votes in the polls being granted the first pick.

VII. PARLIAMENT IN THE NEW ENVIRONMENT

42. In the shared-governance constitution, the executive government will still be accountable to Parliament. However, because of the nature of the decision-making process within the executive (especially its consensus-driven relations), the dynamics of parliament inevitably will change.

43. The parliament will still be required to perform three functions:

- pass legislation and grant statutory powers,
- appropriate and empower government to use public funds, and
- scrutinise and conduct inquiries into the policy, administration and expenditure of government.

44. In Guyana, the same parties that will dominate the government will also dominate the parliament. Given also the existence of strong party control over MPS (partiocracy), the parliament will likely endorse and support the joint decisions of the coalition government. This situation becomes acceptable, as these decisions would have already been processed by inter-party negotiations in the Council of Ministers and in Select Committee where MP's can make their imput. However, there should be provision for MP's (especially regional MP's) not involved in the NEC to dissent.

45. Nevertheless, the structure and functions of parliament should not in any way be weakened or diluted, as it is the only forum for citizens, interest groups, independent MPs, non-government parties and other stakeholders to influence the actions of government. Parliament is also the largest window through which the public can see into the operations of government. In view of this, the following features should supplement the recent constitutional amendments affecting parliament:

46. *Law-making*

All government bills, after their first reading, must be sent to the appropriate select committee for public "hearing of evidence" sessions. Allowances are made for exceptions if:

- the House adopts a motion of the subject Minister that the bill should not go to select committee because it is uncontroversial and no individual or group has formally indicated its intention to give evidence on the bill before the select committee.
- the House adopts a motion of the subject Minister that the bill should not go to select committee because it is urgent.
- the House adopts a motion of the subject Minister that the bill should not go to select committee because prior consultations were held with all interested groups and individuals in drafting the bill, and no other individual or group has formally indicated its intention to give evidence on the bill before the select committee.

47. *Parliamentary debates*

Provisions should be made in the Standing Orders for periodic General Debates in parliament during which MPs could speak on any issue of their own choice.

48. *Public petitions*

The practice of public petitions should be reactivated in Guyana politics. Citizens should be encouraged to submit petitions to parliament on matters affecting them. Select committees would be the forum for processing these petitions and will make recommendations to the full House.

49. *Unresolved coalition matters*

Matters of policy, which the coalition partners are unable to resolve within the Council of Ministers, should be channelled to select committees for public hearings. The committees would then be responsible to seek expert and other opinion on the issue, before making its recommendations to parliament. As discussed above, the matter could be passed by a majority vote of the full House, but would not obligate dissenting parties to shoulder any collective responsibility in that instance.

50. *Select committees*

As envisaged by the recent constitutional amendments, government accountability to the parliament would be mainly actualised through the select committees. In the new environment, it becomes critical that the chairmanship of these committees be opposite to the parties holding responsibility for the corresponding ministries.

VIII. REDEFINITION OF OPPOSITION POLITICS

51. Inevitably, the multiparty government system will redefine opposition politics in Guyana. The political parties, which traditionally would be identified as the opposition, will now be partners in the governing executive. The interparty political debate and discussion, therefore, would no longer be conducted in the public domain but behind the closed doors of the Council of Ministers. The committee recognises that this is an undesirable eventuality, and have proposed steps to, one, open the government decision-making process to public and civic society participation as well as scrutiny.

IX. MECHANISM TO INCREASE PUBLIC AND CIVIC SOCIETY INVOLVEMENT IN NATIONAL DECISION-MAKING

52. To reduce the likelihood of the emergence of executive dictatorship in the new multiparty government, the committee recommends the following ideas:

- Select committee meetings should be in the form of public hearings, bar exceptional circumstances,

- Consultation with stipulated interest groups (regional MPs, trade unions, private sector, municipalities, etc) on major government policies and measures must be mandatory.

X. MEASURES TO INCREASE GOVERNMENT ACCOUNTABILITY

53. As in any democracy, the government must be held accountable to the people. Given the fact that the traditional opposition parties will be in the coalition, the committee recommends the following special provisions to supplement those already enshrined in the constitution.

- Publication of the minutes of meetings of the full cabinet, bar sensitive issues of national security, foreign affairs and trade, "Enactment of Freedom of Information legislation,
- Granting of powers to the president to commission inquiries into government misconduct, and
- More effective and robust government oversight authorities, such as the Auditor General and the constitution commissions, and the redefinition of the scope and powers of the Ombudsman.

XI. CONTROL OF THE MILITARY FORCES

54. The proposed non-executive president will be the Commander-in-Chief of the military. He/she will, however, only act on the advice of the Defence Board, which must include in its composition the leaders of the main political parties in the government.

XII. UNCHANGED PROVISIONS IN THE CONSTITUTION

55. The following constitutional provisions would remain essentially unchanged.

- Provisions for local government,
- Provisions for the establishment of all constitution

commissions,
- Provisions governing individual rights and freedoms,
- Provisions for the independence of the Judiciary and the Auditor General.

XIII. REFERENDUM

56. After a period of ten years, a referendum will be held to determine whether the shared governance arrangement should be continued.

October 16, 2002

APPENDIX 4

TOWARDS GREATER INCLUSIVE GOVERNANCE IN GUYANA

"Building Trust To Achieve Genuine Political Co-operation"
Presented by the PPP/C Government - Posted February 11th.
2003

Pioneering Constitutional Reform and Good Governance

The People's Progressive Party (PPP) was established in 1950
as a multi-ethnic organization with the aim of winning
independence and achieving social justice for all the people
of British Guiana. The founders of the PPP were convinced
of the need for such a Party to involve the broad masses for a
successful challenge to colonialism and to improve the quality
of life of the people. The PPP demanded constitutional reform
with the objective of expanding rights and improving governance
in all its aspects. The PPP was, therefore, a pioneer in the political
campaign for good governance.

The first important victory of the PPP was constitutional
reform allowing for universal adult suffrage for the people of
British Guiana and a ministerial system of Government. After
the first general elections held in 1953, which the PPP won
by a landslide, the improved constitution was suspended and
the colonial authorities persecuted the PPP leaders.

National unity forged by the PPP was shattered by an
engineered division of the Party, which resulted in the formation
of the People's National Congress (PNC).

Despite the division, in all subsequent free and fair elections,
the PPP or the PPP/C won a percentage of votes far larger
than the size of any single ethnic group.

The reason for this consistent success is that the PPP has unwaveringly promoted national unity even in the most difficult days of subversion. The late Leader of the PPP and President of Guyana, Dr. Cheddi Jagan reflects this position in the following statements:

> "Regardless of race or ethnic origin, let us consolidate our forces, win new support and march forward to victory... Racism is the greatest curse of our land... anyone who spreads racial propaganda must be severely dealt with. Such a person is an enemy to himself and his country."
>
> (Dr. Cheddi Jagan, 1965).

> "Unity of the working class regardless of race is vital. If we are to go forward, the party must have the backing not of one race, but of all races. We must take the offensive. We must combat racism mercilessly and build a disciplined party..."
>
> (Dr. Cheddi Jagan, 1967)

The PPP won the 1957 elections after the colonial authorities reinstated constitutional rule. It again succeeded in securing constitutional reform in 1961 when it won elections for the second consecutive time after the suspension of the constitution. It assumed office under an advanced constitution which introduced "self government". The British Government gave the undertaking that independence would be negotiated before the next general elections due in 1965. However, the PPP Government was severely destabilised between 1962 and 1964. The Government was not allowed to serve out its term because of the imposition of early elections with a change in the electoral system from first-past-the-post to proportional representation in order to facilitate the removal of the PPP.

It was as a result of the rejection of efforts towards political unity, increasingly authoritarian rule and elections rigging from 1968 to 1990 that broad unity was sought by the PPP with other opposition forces. The unity which was generated aided the restoration of democracy in 1992 in which the Carter Centre led by Nobel Laureate and former US President Jimmy Carter and other international organizations, including the Commonwealth, played a major role. As a result, the PPP/Civic won the elections and assumed office.

The historical record is unchallengeable: Since the division in 1955, the PPP made continuous efforts to arrive at arrangements with the PNC to maintain and ensure the unity of the Guyanese people. These efforts were particularly intense during the periods 1961 to 1964, 1976 to 1978 and 1984 to 1985. The PNC rejected these efforts categorically describing them at one time as only "superficially attractive."

The struggle for good governance

During the years of authoritarian rule the PPP on its own or in unity with other opposition groups, parties and members of civil society, resisted all efforts to destroy democratic and constitutional rule in Guyana.
    Among the issues which the PPP campaigned against were:

- Elections rigging between 1968 and 1990;
- Abolition of appeals to the Privy Council on constitutional matters
- Politicisation of the Judiciary and Security Forces
- Political and ethnic discrimination
- Abolition of Press Freedom
- Subversion of independent institutions
- Corruption and poor accountability
- Party paramountcy over the institutions and organs of the State
- The 1978 rigged referendum and the 1980 imposed Constitution.

During this period the PPP continually sought unity and explored proposals to generate ethnic security and a restoration of democracy.

The commitment to democracy, constitutional reform and inclusive governance

As a result of the PPP's commitment to democracy it embraced constitutional reform and inclusive and participatory governance as part of its platform for the 1992 general and regional elections. This resulted in the formation of the PPP/Civic alliance to contest those elections.

Upon its accession to office in October 1992, the PPP/Civic Government inherited one of the poorest and most heavily indebted countries in the hemisphere with, inter alia:

- Over 90 percent of revenue being used to service external debt;
- Over 60 percent of the population living below the poverty line;
- Severe macro-economic imbalances including a fiscal deficit of 25 percent of GDP and a balance of payments deficit of 47 percent of GDP;
- High interest rates;
- Runaway inflation;
- Dilapidated physical and social infrastructure;
- Lack of public accountability; and
- Mass migration leading to a severe "brain drain"

Today, the debt servicing is less than 40 percent of revenue, the population below the poverty line has been reduced by half, the balance of payments and fiscal deficits are below 10 percent of GDP, interest rates have been cut in half and for the last eight years inflation is in single digits. The physical and social infrastructure has been significantly rehabilitated. In addition, the Government has made significant progress in advancing good governance and financial accountability through the introduction of the following measures:

- Return of and respect for democratic norms;
- Independent functioning of State institutions;
- Expansion of press freedom;
- Participation of the Opposition on state boards;
- Amendment of the Standing Orders of the National Assembly to allow for Standing Committees;
- Reintroduction of financial accountability especially through the submission of annual reports of the public accounts by the Auditor General;

– Reform of the tendering process;
– Appointment of the Integrity Commission;
– Introduction of legislation to prevent discrimination and
  marginalisation at the work place;
– Fair and transparent financial and resource allocation to
  regions, sectors and communities.

The PPP/C Government's attempts to establish a Race
Relations Commission failed due to the lack of opposition
support.

The achievements set out above are not exhaustive but a
mere indication of the substantial work done by the PPP/C
Government to restore good governance and participatory
democracy to Guyana.

Constitutional reform commenced during the Cheddi Jagan
Government by the appointment of a Select Committee on which
the Opposition was represented. The Select Committee travelled
to many parts of the country and compiled several volumes of
evidence. However, it was unable to conclude its report and
make its recommendations because Parliament was dissolved
and elections called for December, 1997.

Constitutional Reform and Inclusive Governance

In 1997, the PPP/C won the elections, which were certified
as free and fair by international observers. Once again sustained
destablisation activities created instability, threatened social peace
and obstructed the functioning of government offices. In order
to ensure that the situation did not spin out of control, the
PPP/C agreed to major compromises in the Herdmanston
Accord. The Government's term of office was reduced by two
years, it agreed to an audit of the elections and undertook to
continue the process of constitutional reform.

The Audit concluded that the elections were free and fair.

A Constitutional Reform Commission was established and
the PPP/C agreed to substantial reforms that advance the process
of inclusive governance.

The Constitution was amended to provide for:

(a) Reducing the powers of the President;

(b) An Opposition veto on the appointment of the Chancellor and Chief Justice;

(c) Expanding the functions of the Judicial Service Commission;

(d) Strengthening the financial independence of the Judiciary and Auditor General;

(e) Institutionalising participation by social groups in the decision making process;

(f) Expanding human rights;

(g) Involving the National Assembly in the appointment of Service Commissions (Public, Police, Judicial and Teaching);

(h) Modifying the electoral system for national and local government elections;

(i) Establishing of five Standing Committees to examine and review government policy in the social, economic, foreign policy and natural resources sectors;

(j) A Parliamentary Management Committee;

(k) A Human Rights Commission;

(l) An Ethnic Relations Commission; a Procurement Commission;

(m) A Standing Committee on Constitutional Reform;

(n) A Commission to review the functioning and composition of the security forces; and

(o) Commissions on the Rights of the Child, Gender Rights and Indigenous Peoples.

(p) These and other reforms make the Guyana Constitution the most advanced in terms of inclusiveness and Opposition involvement in governance in the Caribbean region and certainly one of the most advanced in the world.

The Human Rights, Ethnic Relations and Procurement Commissions established in a bi-partisan way together can address allegations of police excesses, ethnic discrimination and corruption, which are some of the main unsubstantiated accusations which the Opposition has levelled against the Government. However, these and the other reforms now provided for by the Constitution to deal with these issues have not been given effect to because of the current boycott of Parliament by the Opposition.

In addition to the above, the constitutional standing committees of Parliament and the Parliamentary Management Committee have not been established nor have the commissions on social groups, which include commissions on Rights of the Child, Gender Rights and Indigenous People.

The PPP/C once again won the 2001 general elections under a modified electoral system. These elections were certified as free and fair by international observers, including the Carter Centre, the Commonwealth, the OAS, the European Union and CARICOM. Immediately after the conclusion of the elections, the PNC/R opposition organized extensive protest demonstrations.

Consistent with the PPP and the Government's position on dialogue, as stated by President Bharrat Jagdeo below, an invitation was issued to the late Mr. Desmond Hoyte, then Leader of the PNC/R to dialogue.

"I extend a hand of friendship to those who are in opposition and invite them to sit with us and iron out differences so that we can have a common cause to serve – a cause in service to our people and nation".
(President Jagdeo, August 11, 1999)

"It is critical that we engage one another in dialogue. We should always reach out and talk to each other. In this way, we would be fulfilling the mandate of all Guyanese as we share our differing views in the search for national consensus on the common objective of making this country a better place for all".
(President Jagdeo, March 31, 2001)

Arising from the agreements, the following bi-partisan committees were established:

– Local government reform;
– Border and national security;
– Distribution of land and houselots;

– Resuscitation of the bauxite industry;
– Depressed communities' needs; and
– Radio monopoly and non-partisan boards

The achievements of the dialogue included:

a) Depressed Communities Needs Committee: Four areas were identified by the Committee: Non Pariel/Enterprise, Buxton, De Kinderen and Meten-eer-Zorg. The Government had set aside $60M to do work in these areas. The agreed development work has been carried out in all of the four communities.

b) The Report of Border and National Security Committee: The committee met on a number of occasions and produced a report. President Jagdeo and Mr. Hoyte met with members of the committee and agreed that the report will be tabled in the National Assembly for the consideration of the Sectoral Committee on Foreign Affairs when it is formed.

c) National Policy on Distribution of Land and House lots: Both President Jagdeo and Mr. Hoyte rejected the report of the Committee on the distribution of land and house lots. It was agreed that the Government would table a white paper on land distribution and the criteria for selection by the end of February 2002. However Parliament did not meet until March 15th, 2002. The White Paper was tabled.

d) The Bauxite Industry Resuscitation Committee: On February 19, 2002, President Jagdeo and Mr. Hoyte met with the members of the Bauxite Resuscitation Committee. It was agreed that it would focus on the LINMINE privatisation issue. A negotiating team comprising representatives from the Government and the Opposition would be set up to engage OMAI/Cambior for the privatisation of LINMINE. On February 19th, 2002, Mr. Hoyte was asked to submit his representative, which he subsequently did. This has resulted in a MoU between the Government of Guyana and Omai/Cambior.

e) The Report of the Radio Monopoly and Non-partisan

Media Boards: The report was presented to President Jagdeo and Mr. Hoyte. It was noted that no agreement was reached on the issue of the National Frequency Management Unit (NFMU) at the committee level. On February 18th, 2002, Mr. Hoyte suggested to President Jagdeo that the Government of Guyana proceed with the drafting of necessary legislation pending agreement on the issue of the NFMU. By February 19th, 2002, President Jagdeo had informed Mr. Hoyte that the report was sent to the Attorney General Chambers so that the drafting process could start. It would be useful to note that on November 7th, 2001, President Jagdeo and Mr. Hoyte signed a Memorandum of Understanding, which cleared the way for the passage of the amendment to the Wireless Telegraphy Regulations (which was agreed to by the joint committee) and the establishment of an interim Advisory Committee on Broadcasting with respect to compliance by television stations licensees.

(f) Local Government Reform Committee: The Joint Task force on Local Government Reform has made tremendous progress up to the time its mandate expired on May 18th, 2002. The Committee has made a request for an extension of the mandate by three months, so that it could wind up its work.

Other progress made by the dialogue included:

PNC/R Membership on State Boards, Commission and Committees: Mr. Hoyte had raised the issue of PNC/R participation on boards. As a result, PNC/R nominees were named to serve on over 50 state boards, commissions and committees.

1. Creation of post of Head of the Public Service: President Jagdeo and Mr. Hoyte agreed "to create a position of a formal Head of the Public Service separate and distinct from the political post of Head of the Presidential Secretariat."
2. Parliamentary Management Committee and Sectoral

Committees: At the February 18 and 19th, 2002 dialogue meetings, the President, once again, suggested to Mr. Hoyte that since their representatives (Messrs Persaud and Carberry) were unable to reach agreement on the issue, they should discuss this outstanding matter at their level. Mr. Hoyte, in response, suggested that the matter should be dealt with at a subsequent meeting.

3. On March 14, 2002, the PNCR surprisingly, put the dialogue on pause despite the above achievements alleging that agreements were not fulfilled.

Building Trust

Post-independence politics in Guyana has been characterized by a lack of trust between the two main political parties despite the determined efforts of the PPP and the PPP/C.

Recently, executive power sharing has been proposed as a solution to Guyana's problems. Quite apart from the negative consequences associated with executive power sharing such as the institutionalisation of ethnic rivalry and the absence of political opposition, no contrived system of governance will succeed in a situation where trust and good faith do not exist between the political parties.

The PPP/C believes that a conscious effort is required by the major political parties to build trust and establish confidence. Without such trust, suspicion will continue, motives will be questioned, policies will be judged on distorted criteria, resource allocation will always be followed by allegations of partisanship and agreements will be difficult to be arrived at. It is not even possible at this time to sign a crime communiqué as proposed by the Social Partners.

The PPP/C proposes the implementation of all the constitutional reforms as an immediate measure to building trust and to further enhance inclusive governance. In this regard, the parties will be required to collaborate on:

– the appointment of the Rights Commissions;

– the appointment of the Parliamentary Management
   Committee;
– the appointment of the Service Commissions; and
– the appointment of the Standing Committees.

The establishment of these and other bodies provided for
in the Constitution and their optional functioning will generate
confidence and increasing co-operation and goodwill.

The PPP/C will expand on these efforts by encouraging broader
co-operation by all forces in the society involved in public affairs
but particularly the political parties.

These collaborative efforts would include:

(a) establishing means and facilities to enhance the work
    of Members of Parliament and strengthening their ability
    to present their views in legislative matters and to represent
    their constituents.
(b) improving the discourse between Government and
    Opposition through the appointment of Shadow Cabinet
    Ministers who can represent their views on policy to the
    Government and be apprised of policy developments by
    the Government.
(c) improving ties between the political parties through
    discussions and debates which will also contribute to
    building confidence.
(d) devising additional ways and means of working closer
    together in a non-partisan way at the local government
    level where national political controversies generate less
    divisions and where development and implementation
    issues give rise to the possibility of greater co-operation
    in the short term.

These measures which are vital for our political development
and the emergence of a new political culture characterized by
greater trust, civility and commitment to the national interest.

The PPP/C is encouraged by recent pronouncements by the
main opposition party which indicate a commitment for
constructive engagement. We hope that these engagements will

result in the acceptance of these and other proposals to solve national issues, to build trust and to improve relations between our political parties.

In an environment created by deepening trust and confidence, further arrangements for inclusive governance can result after consultation with our constituents and the electorate.

APPENDIX   5

THE NATIONAL DEVELOPMENT STRATEGY– A SUMMARY.[1]

The National development Strategy (NDS) sets out priorities for our nation's economic and social development for the next decade. The draft document – which is made up six volumes – contains careful technical analysis of problems and future prospects in all sectors of the economy and in areas of social concern. It presents us with an opportunity to work together to prepare Guyana for the challenges of the next century.

The draft NDS – which was launched on Monday 6th January, 1997 by the late President His Excellency Dr Cheddi Jagan – is a result of over 300 hours of meetings by 23 "technical working groups" consisting of over 200 Guyanese. These efforts were co-ordinated by the Ministry of Finance, but the contributors came from a wide cross-section of organisations including the private sector, government agencies, non-government agencies, and the University of Guyana. The Carter Center assisted the Ministry of Finance with the overall co-ordination of the exercise.

This article summarises the key recommendations made by the NDS in the areas of macroeconomics (Volume 2), the social sectors (Volume 3), the productive sectors (Volume 4) and the infrastructure sectors (Volume 5). We encourage you to read the summaries and send your comments and recommendations to the NDS Secretariat, Ministry of Finance, Main Street, Georgetown (Tel: 02-67242; Fax: 02-73458).

THE MACROECONOMIC STRATEGY (VOLUME 2)

The macroeconomic strategy put forward in the NDS is directly concerned with economic growth, employment, the distribution of income, inflation, poverty and sustainability in fiscal, environmental and institutional terms.

Principal Macroeconomic Issues and Constraints

In this chapter, the NDS looks at the issues and constraints facing Guyana at the level of the economy as a whole, such as the level of debt, the lack of competitiveness of several of the country's exports, and the weaknesses in the public sector. In some respects, a number of improvements have occurred in the economy, including a reduction in inflation, smaller "fiscal deficits" (the gap between government expenditure and revenue), higher foreign exchange reserves, and a stronger banking system. The NDS identifies some remaining problems:

- a high level of external debt. A number of debt relief initiatives have reduced Guyana's debt to its donors. However, debt payments remain high, which severely squeezes the funding for vital infrastructure, social services, and salaries in the public sector. The NDS calls for continued lobbying for additional debt relief and other debt reduction measures.
- uncertainty over preferential access to rice and sugar markets. This is serious given the importance of these sectors and the fact that many of the producers are currently unable to compete at the world market price. The NDS recommends continued lobbying for the maintenance of preferential markets, and various strategies to modernise operations and improve competitiveness.
- a lack of competitiveness of several of Guyana's exports. The NDS calls for a reduction in import tariffs, as well as reforms in the banking sector to ease exporters' access to credit and foreign exchange.
- a need for the clarification and strengthening of the

incentive regime for private sector investment. The NDS recommends a clear investment code that provides comparable treatment to investors in all sectors; the simplification and greater transparency of the investment approval process; and a review of consumption taxes and customs duties, so that different products and sectors are treated more equitably. The NDS also calls for the acceleration of the privatisation process.

- very low levels of pay in the public service, resulting in staff shortages (especially at the management levels) and an inadequately skilled workforce. The low level of pay is linked to the government's narrow revenue base. In addition to measures to increase government revenues, the NDS recommends the progressive improvement of salaries in the public sector; reforms to the budgeting system; and a more focused role for the government. The NDS suggests that by concentrating on guidance through policies, the government can make the best contribution to economic growth.

Principal Orientations of Macroeconomic Policy

The objectives of macroeconomic policy for the next ten years can be summarised as follows:

- Promote continuing high growth rates of output and employment.
- Ensure that inflation remains at relatively low levels.
- Ensure that the population's basic needs are met and that the growth process contributes to a reduction in poverty.
- Ensure that the growth path is sustainable in fiscal, environmental and institutional terms.

In order to meet these objectives, it will be necessary to meet a number of sub-objectives:

- enhance the institutional and financial effectiveness of

the public sector to fulfil its roles and responsibilities.
- adopt policies that encourage exports and improvements in the international competitiveness of Guyana's producing sectors.
- continue to improve the efficiency of the banking system, to promote both savings and investment.
- promote policies that enhance the role of the private sector in the economy and encourage greater levels of participation in decisions related to economic development and economic management on the part of families, communities, associations, and local governments.

The External Sector and Monetary Management

The principal objectives of the NDS in this area are to promote the growth of output and employment and to keep inflation at low levels. The NDS recommends:

- strategies to support the development of international trade. The NDS suggests, for example, the creation of an Export Processing Zone (EPZ) which will provide substantial employment opportunities, export earnings and foreign exchange. The NDS also calls for a review of the fiscal regime; the improvement of the system of agricultural research to give sectors such as rice the opportunity to enhance their technologies and become more competitive; the restructuring of GO-INVEST to separate its investment promotion function from its investment approval function; and the strengthening of technical vocational education and training (TVET) facilities to enhance to the supply of skilled labour.
- measures to ensure an appropriate exchange rate.
- the maintenance of the government's "monetary policy", as it relates to interest rates, the supply of money, inflation and legislation concerning the banking sector, the Bank of Guyana and the financial markets.

Fiscal Policy and the Public Sector

In this chapter, the NDS looks at appropriate policies relating to government spending and revenue, as well as at the problems faced in the public sector. The NDS recommends:

- the continued reduction of fiscal deficits. Domestic borrowing to pay for the excess of spending over revenues received causes prices and interest rates to rise. This, in turn, reduces the rate of private sector investment. Therefore, it is important to limit and prioritise expenditures and enhance revenues.
- the prioritisation of expenditure on basic social needs for health, education, poverty alleviation and social infrastructure such as potable water and sewerage systems. Other priorities should be productive infrastructure (especially transport and electricity) and public sector salaries. In addition, the NDS recommends that subsidies and transfers should be well targeted on social priorities.
- the enhancement of revenues, through a review of the fiscal regime, the broadening of the tax base, improved collection and staff training. The NDS stresses the importance of implementing the Revenue Authority. The incorporation of the Inland Revenue Department and the Customs and Excise Department into one body should reduce administrative inefficiency, informational gaps, and the overlapping of responsibilities. The NDS also supports the proposed computerised Unique Tax Identification Number to facilitate the sharing of information between agencies.
- the examination of the feasibility of introducing value added tax (VAT). With the move to a lower Common External Tariff (for CARICOM countries), it will be important to move away from consumption and import taxes in order to maintain current levels of revenue.
- the reduction of the high staff vacancies in the public sector. This will require action on wages; the NDS recognises that the issue of wages must be tackled before

any other reforms can be properly implemented. In addition to consolidating some of the vacancies into more highly-skilled positions, the NDS calls for a review of the size of the public sector in line with its role; the development of a transparent pay policy, an incentive structure, performance evaluations, and clear disciplinary procedures; the introduction of retraining schemes to enable staff to fill vacancies at higher levels; and, the training of managers in the management of change.

- the improvement of expenditure management, including the ending of the separation of capital and current expenditure management; the move to "programme budgeting" which rationalises expenditures based on programme objectives and results; the continued computerisation of the budget process; and, a recognition of the important links between resource utilisation and the NDS.

- the adoption of a more clearly defined and focused role for the government. The NDS sees the private sector as the engine for growth, employment and higher incomes. It is recommended that the government focus mainly on assuring the provision of basic social services and infrastructure, and that it strengthens its regulatory and monitoring role, especially in the areas of natural resource development and the financial sector. Above all, the government should ensure that the basic needs of the poorest groups in the population are met.

- the continuation of the privatisation programme. This is recommended by the NDS as part of the greater emphasis on the private sector. The NDS also suggests the establishment of an updated regulatory framework for newly privatised utilities.

Debt Management

Guyana faces high debt payments for both domestic and external debt, despite declining interest rates (in the case of domestic debt) and recent debt write offs (in the case of external). This has resulted in a reduction in the resources available for important expenditures, such as social infrastructure. The NDS recommends:

- strategies to deal with the domestic debt, including strengthened management of the money supply and the use of appropriate levels of "treasury bills" (on which the government must pay interest); prudent fiscal and monetary policies to lower inflation; and reductions in fiscal deficits and the level of domestic debt.
- strategies to deal with the external debt, including policies to accelerate economic growth (to reduce the relative size of the debt); further efforts to obtain debt write-offs; the paying off of some non-concessional debts with concessional borrowing; and various mechanisms to reduce the cost of debt servicing.

Banking Policy

The NDS seeks to promote the viability of the banking system while preserving competitiveness and a sound financial environment. The commercial banks and other financial intermediaries play an important economic role, such as by mobilising savings for investment purposes. The NDS recommends:

- an improvement of accounting and disclosure standards, to ensure the harmonisation of practices across different banks (including local operations of foreign-based banks).
- the introduction of regulations to prevent credit concentration (where significant amounts are lent to a few borrowers) and the associated risk, as well as regulations concerning provisioning for bad debts, in order to maintain the stability of the financial system.
- the establishment of a Legal Review Committee to look at existing financial laws and identify areas of obscurity

and uncertainty, and to make recommendations for tighter enforcement of contracts.

- the strengthening of the Bank of Guyana's ability to supervise financial institutions. This will require legislative reforms to provide it with sufficient legal powers.
- the involvement of Guyana in the consideration of a Regional Stock Exchange for the Eastern Caribbean.

THE SOCIAL SECTORS (VOLUME 3)

Social policies are given a central place in the National Development Strategy (NDS); Volume III (The Social Sectors) is the largest of the six volumes of the NDS. Social policies are crucial to satisfying the national objectives of poverty alleviation, satisfaction of basic social and economic needs, and sustainment of a democratic and fully participatory society.

Poverty Alleviation/Reduction

Despite recent improvements, poverty remains a critical issue for many people in Guyana. The NDS has four priorities for poverty alleviation:

- the need to promote rapid and sustainable economic growth in a labour-intensive manner, since this expands employment opportunities and raises income levels. As exports are generally the most labour-intensive products, they should be promoted through, for example, an export processing zone.
- the need to increase the productivity of the poor. For the poor to truly benefit from these employment opportunities, emphasis must be placed on formal and non-formal education and training, improved access to land for small farmers, and enhanced access to credit for micro and small enterprises.
- reform of the institutional structure and operating procedures of social safety nets. Until everyone is able to meet their own basic needs, effective social safety nets

targeted at the poor must remain a priority. The NDS also recommends the strengthening of the relevant Government agencies, and sees an important role for non-government organisations.

- policy reforms to replace generalised subsidies with ones that are targeted on the poor. Recognising that resources are not available for addressing all the problems of all groups immediately, the NDS suggests that priority be given to women and children, youth, senior citizens, the disabled, and the Amerindian communities.

Environmental Policy

Environmental issues affect the health, well-being and future of the people of Guyana. The environmental policies of the NDS intend to promote the sustainable management of natural resources and preserve a healthy environment in coastal, urban and hinterland regions:

- The NDS is strongly in favour of the Environmental Protection Agency as a body to focus on issues such as, the management of renewable resources, environmental degradation, agricultural and industrial pollution, public awareness and legislation.
- In coastland areas, the NDS calls for the rehabilitation and maintenance of the sea defences and irrigation infrastructure, as well as protection of the mangroves.
- In urban areas, the NDS recommends strategies to deal with waste management and pollution.
- And for the hinterland, the NDS supports a National Forestry Code of Practice and a similar set of standards for the mining sector; the use of "environmental impact assessments" for forestry and mining operations; the development of non-timber uses of forests; the promotion of "ecotourism"; and the establishment of a system of protected areas to preserve Guyana's unique biological diversity.

Health Policy

The objectives of the NDS are to improve the population's access to health care and the quality of that health care. Throughout, the aim is to ensure that no-one is denied access to health care because they are unable to pay. Recommendations include:

- improvements to the referral system alongside improvements in local health care facilities. It is also suggested that the Ministry of Health becomes the sole health authority in the public sector, and that individual hospitals are given greater autonomy.
- improvements in the supply, management and distribution of drugs and medical supplies.
- increased investment in primary health care (with the establishment of a primary health care division in the Ministry of Health). It is suggested that efforts be made to improve hinterland access to primary health care, and that overall priority be given to children, adolescents, and pregnant or lactating women.
- the tackling of the staffing and resource constraints in the sector.
- the upgrade of air and water ambulances and an expanded programme of rotating physician visits to some of the more remote communities.
- the encouragement of private medical personnel to practice in hinterland areas.

Educational Policy

The NDS recommends strategies to boost the levels of literacy and numeracy in the population and improve the availability of all levels of education from pre-school care and nursery, to technical vocational education and training (TVET), adult education and university. The NDS recommends:

- increases in funding, particularly for the primary level - which faces the greatest constraints, and yet has the greatest payoffs for economic development. In addition, it is suggested that regional variations in expenditure be reduced.
- increases in teachers' salaries and the introduction of performance incentives.
- improvements in teacher training (including for special needs education) through the setting up of new training centres.
- improved targeting of subsidies.
- encouragement of private sector and non-government organisation involvement in the provision of education and training.
- the development by the University of Guyana of a long-term plan for establishing centres of excellence in areas such as tropical forestry and forest management, geology and mining, and fisheries management.

Women, Gender and Development

This chapter of the NDS looks at the situation of Guyanese women in terms of poverty, employment, health, education, the household, and the media. Recommendations are made to tackle the higher incidence of poverty amongst women, the difficulties women face in the work place (such as low pay), the high incidence of domestic violence, and the specific health problems they face (including malnutrition and high maternal mortality). Specific suggestions include:

- the promotion of microenterprises and the creation of a national credit institution.
- investment in distance learning education and training in non-traditional (and higher paying) fields.
- the introduction of "family-friendly" working environments (through such things as "flexi-time", child care facilities at work, and maternal and paternal leave).

- increased investment in social services.
- strengthening of the Women Affairs Bureau alongside the establishment of a National Commission on Women that will recommend and lobby for policy reforms.
- a greater role for the media in raising public awareness, as well as enhancing women's understanding of their legal rights.

Amerindian Policies

The NDS seeks to tackle issues facing Amerindians in the areas of land, poverty and education. Recommendations are made to tackle Amerindians' marginalisation in the development process:

- reforms to secure Amerindian land rights. Those communities affected by resource development and extraction should share in the benefits.
- the expansion of the Amerindian Development Fund. It is recommended that funds be spent on community development projects and training.
- increased investment in health facilities, schools and training centres, as well as improvements to salaries of personnel working in hinterland areas.
- the development of more relevant curricula in schools.
- the strengthening of the Ministry of Amerindian Affairs.

Urban Development and the Housing Sector

The main objective is to improve access to housing, basic services and amenities in Guyana's cities. The sector faces a lack of adequate planning; human and financial resource shortages; a scarcity of land for housing; and poor water and sewerage systems. The NDS recommends:

- strategies to increase the supply of housing. One suggestion is to make land available in freehold to entrepreneurs who will commit to constructing housing on the lots, while the Government commits to supplying the necessary infrastructure services. It is suggested also that the Government supply serviced lots to needy families.
- policies to enhance the capacity of lower and middle income groups to purchase and rent housing. One method would be the use of rental and mortgage supplements for low income families. In the case of State land occupied by squatters, an option would be to grant freehold title in exchange for a supplemented mortgage.
- the strengthening of the municipalities.
- the development of export processing zones and industrial estates to generate employment in urban areas.
- the allocation of land to the greenbelts to curtail urban sprawl.

The Role of Regional and Local Government

The objective of the NDS is to create a more decentralised framework of regional and local government. Recommendations include:

- the clarification of the structure, roles and responsibilities of the Regional Democratic Councils, the Neighbourhood Democratic Councils and the numerous other levels of local government.
- various administrative and legislative reforms to give a greater degree of autonomy to regional and local government.
- the streamlining of the local government structure and the strengthening of regional and local agencies through staff training and improvements in the budgeting system.

THE PRODUCTIVE SECTORS (VOLUME 4)

Agriculture and Forestry

Agriculture is the single most important sector of Guyana's economy; more that 70% of Guyana's population live in rural households and are primarily dependent on income generated from agriculture and related activities.

Rice Development

Rice is Guyana's second major crop and a major source of income, employment and foreign exchange. Despite improvements since the late 1980s, the rice sector continues to face a number of constraints that hinder its development. The NDS makes the following suggestions to address problems such as, the lack of competitiveness on the international market, inadequate access to credit and land (especially for small farmers), and institutional weaknesses:

- strengthen the Guyana Rice Development Board (GRDB), in terms of its ability to conduct forward looking analysis; regulate contractual procedures, payment mechanisms and rice quality; and raise revenue from sources other than export taxes, which decrease the competitiveness of the sector.
- reinvest the benefits from Guyana's preferential export markets back into the rice sector to improve competitiveness. The rice sector may find itself in a precarious position if and when the preferential markets provided by the "Lomé IV Convention" are lost or reduced. Efforts should centre on focusing the sector on the CARICOM market; rehabilitating infrastructure, such as wharf facilities, water channels, and D&I; the creation of a deep water harbour; and diversification within the rice sector.
- increase productivity and promote technology development by, for example, improving access to credit for both millers

and producers. The NDS also calls for the promotion of research, based on market demands and the experiences of farmers, to look at productivity, yield variability, pest control, and the development of characteristics demanded by the export and domestic markets.

The Sugar Industry

Historically, the sugar industry has played an important social and economic role within Guyana. Today, it is the largest single employer in the country. The NDS makes recommendations to reduce its high production costs and increase its competitiveness; particularly important given the likely reduction in the preferential prices Guyana receives through the European Union:

- continue lobbying for the maintenance of preferential markets. There is currently uncertainty over preferential access to sugar markets. This is serious given the importance of this sector in the economy and the fact that less efficient estates are currently unable to compete at the world market price.
- invest in the modernisation of the industry and reduce recurrent production costs. The NDS calls for a thoroughgoing review of the industry's cost structure.
- pursue policies to improve the sector's competitiveness, including an appropriate exchange rate policy.
- strategies to enhance the financing, management and efficiency of the sector, such as through a participatory privatisation involving workers.

Other Agriculture

Non-traditional crops are labour intensive and generate substantial levels of foreign exchange. Promoting the output of this sector will, therefore, increase rural incomes, employment and foreign exchange earnings, and reduce rural poverty. The NDS recommends:

- the development of land and infrastructure. As part of this effort, the Lands and Surveys Department should be strengthened to enable it to improve its surveying capability, provide more efficient services to farmers, and co-ordinate with other land management agencies. Government should also ensure reliable electricity and potable water supplies to rural districts. In addition, it is suggested that participatory programmes be developed for the operation and maintenance of drainage and irrigation schemes.
- the focusing of research on selected commodities and certain geographic zones based on marketability and production potential. The Ministry of Agriculture should focus on developing agronomic programmes for crop varieties that have assured markets, taking into consideration their applicability to existing farming conditions and the varying economic resources of farmers. It is also suggested that plant protection and quarantine services be improved.
- the encouragement of private sector involvement in the sector through workshops, the creation of a computerised information centre, and the reintroduction of the National Science Research Council. Private sector involvement should also be encouraged in agricultural extension.
- the assistance of farmers in accessing credit. For example, the government should support rural development centres and agricultural co-operatives which can assist farmers in preparing proposals to credit agencies.
- the establishment of an advisory services agency that informs farmers of market opportunities, assists in finding inputs and obtaining access to markets, and directs farmers' concerns to relevant agencies. One option is marketing centres managed by the private sector.
- the promotion of agriculture as a core subject in school curricula. Learning institutions should be better equipped

and practical agricultural training must be emphasised.
- the introduction of strategies to promote livestock nutrition and health, including the development of energy based and protein feeds production; improvement of the productivity of saline and acid soils to ensure adequate pasturage; and strengthening of abattoir and veterinarian services, financed partly by cost-recovery measures.

The Institutional Framework for Agriculture

The institutional framework for the agriculture sector is made up of various agencies ranging from the Ministry of Agriculture and the National Agricultural Research Institute (NARI) to the producer organisations and Neighbourhood Democratic Councils (NDCs). The NDS makes a number of recommendations to deal with the constraints these agencies face, such as limited financial and human resources; weak linkages between national agencies; a weak policy review capacity; and a lack of decentralisation:

- the development of a plan by the Ministry of Agriculture for the future direction of agricultural support services, which would prioritise government functions and provide measures for the development of the small farm sector.
- the provision of financial support for the development of the small farm sector by, for example, targeting a proportion of the preferential gains from rice and sugar exports; introducing higher rentals of State land and taxes on freehold; and initiating a system of charges for larger farms for extension services.
- the strengthening of local level institutions, such as the Neighbourhood Democratic Councils, non-government organisations, and producer organisations. It is suggested that the Government grant NDCs greater scope in the determination of resource use, and provide technical training in legal issues, management, finance, budgeting and resource mobilisation.

- the introduction of Government incentives to encourage banks to locate branches in rural areas, and the consideration by banks of group lending schemes.

Agricultural Land Policy

The NDS makes recommendations to promote rapid growth through improvements in the efficiency with which land resources are used, and to support poverty alleviation by increasing access to land for the landless and small rural farmers:

- improve leasing practices by, for example, developing clear selection criteria for approval and denial of leasing applications; ensuring both the land selection committee and the regional committee be comprised of elected members; and speeding up the approval process.
- formulate a standard agricultural lease with provisions for 99 or 999 year limits; transferability after 5 years; the ability to use leased lands as collateral or to sublet leased land without the approval of the lessor; and the option to convert to freehold after 10 to 15 years beneficial leasehold.
- annually adjust land rental rates to market values, with special provisions made for the rural poor. The revenue generated by the new rent levels should be re-invested back into improved land administration and agricultural development.
- promote better utilisation of freehold agricultural lands by eliminating unnecessary restrictions on land rental practices; and introducing a rural land tax (to discourage underutilisation of land).
- design a National Land Use Plan to define sustainable land use practices, targeting areas in need of reforestation or suitable for long-term agricultural development. The Plan should give special priority to benefiting the indigenous population, and deterring illegal occupancy of reservation lands.

Forest Management

The forest industry represents vast economic potential for Guyana. The NDS makes recommendations to increase the economic benefits derived from the forests; improve the sustainability of the sector; and spread the benefits of forest-based development to Guyana's rural areas:

- conduct a review of forest fees.
- develop a policy framework for concessions that will make the process more transparent; protect the rights of the investors; and enable the enforcement of their obligations. The policy will address the location and size of the new forest management concessions; the length of tenure; questions of transferability; the sustainable use of forests for non-timber products and nature tourism; and log exporting.
- encourage labour-intensive wood processing industries through fiscal incentives.
- strengthen and streamline the Guyana Forestry Commission (GFC). The GFC should focus on sustainable forest management and move away from commercial marketing of forest products. The NDS also recommends granting the GFC more autonomy with regards to raising revenue. A new organisation, with a board made up from the private and public sectors, should be set up to provide marketing and product development support, research and training.

Fisheries Policy

The NDS aims to maintain and improve the nutritional, social and economic benefits from the fisheries sector in a sustainable manner. The following recommendations are made:

- support artisanal fishermen by improving cold-storage and processing facilities and the marketing system.

- strengthen Guyana's fisheries management system (such as the Department of Fisheries and the Coast Guard) to promote a sustainable use of fish stocks; improve the enforcement of regulations; accurately assess current stocks; enhance the extension system; and improve quality control to strengthen export potential. It is suggested that the Department of Fisheries be reorganised and reinstituted as an autonomous Guyana Fisheries Commission.
- focus efforts more towards deep water finfish, and introduce strategies to limit fishing of marine prawn and seabob to sustainable levels. Regulations for gear types should be introduced.
- develop a policy for the long-term development of the aquaculture sector, which is the sub-sector of fisheries with the greatest potential for expansion of production, creation of employment, and generation of foreign exchange. Improvements in access to freehold land or secure leases of a reasonably long duration will be necessary. Expansion of aquaculture activities in shrimp production may be an important way to sustainably manage shrimp populations, and maximise their export potential.

THE PRODUCTIVE SECTORS CONT'D (VOLUME 4)

Non-Agriculture

Outside agriculture, there are various important productive sectors that are addressed in the NDS. This section summarises some of the recommendations made. Also discussed is the policy framework for the private sector, which applies to all the productive sectors.

Policy Framework for the Private Sector

In the NDS, a central challenge has been finding the most appropriate ways of combining the power of market forces, as the primary impulses to development, with the role of the State in providing the development framework, monitoring the process, and providing special assistance to target groups. The NDS makes various recommendations to ensure that the private sector continues to play a key role in the growth of the economy and that it is the major engine of employment creation and improved living conditions:

- the provision of infrastructural support to the private sector by the government.
- a focus by the government on upgrading the human resources of the economy through education and training, as well as through the provision of basic social services.
- the development of a definitive national policy aimed at stimulating investments, industrial performance and commercial development. The government should involve the private sector in this process.
- a review of the tax system, especially with respect to consumption tax and import tariffs, in order to facilitate private sector production planning and investment. The NDS also suggests considering the feasibility of a value-added tax (VAT) as a replacement for consumption tax.
- the setting up of Export Processing Zones (EPZs) to promote and facilitate investment, as well as to create employment and generate foreign exchange.
- the publication and wide distribution of a clear and simplified investment code. It is recommended that a "one-stop" investment approval office be established to improve the current time-consuming approval process. It is also suggested that a separate entity, made up of representatives of the public and private sector, be set up to deal with investment promotion.
- the improvement of the information database on external markets and market niches, so as to assist the private sector to search for new markets, in addition to the domestic market and CARICOM. The NDS also urges that the government support the private sector by sharing information on the availability of development aid and technical assistance.

Mining Policy

Despite the decline of the bauxite industry, mineral development has the potential to once again become an engine for economic growth in Guyana. The NDS makes several recommendations to deal with the constraints experienced in all subsectors of mining, and to ensure the continued growth of the mining sector as a whole:

- the enhancement of the mining policy so that it embraces a fiscal regime, marketing arrangements, policies on technology, security of titles, training, the environment, and an approach to social issues in mining communities.
- the encouragement of infrastructure development related to mining. The high cost of transportation and lack of essential services in the hinterland often deters foreign direct investment.
- a review of the fiscal regime. Specifically, the NDS calls for a review of royalties, export duties, and income taxes. It also suggests the introduction of fiscal incentives to encourage technology that is environmentally friendly.
- the replacement of the Guyana Gold Board with a system of licensed and bonded gold buyers who will be responsible for remitting royalties to the Government.
- the strengthening of the Guyana Geology and Mines Commission (GGMC). The GGMC needs to commission a national mineral resource inventory, continue to explore state of the art mining and milling technologies, and construct a modern integrated laboratory for relevant analysis and testing.
- the establishment of a commission to reconsider land rental policies.
- the development of a programme for the bauxite industry, including the privatisation of BERMINE and LINMINE.

The Manufacturing Sector

Guyana's abundant endowment of natural resources provides an important basis for manufacturing development. However, for the growth of this sector to be realised, a number of constraints need to be addressed. The NDS makes recommendations to promote the rapid increase of production and employment in the sector:

- the creation of at least one Export Processing Zone (EPZ), located in close proximity to deepwater harbour facilities and to the Linden-Lethem road link.
- the development of adequate social and physical infrastructure. In addition to the improvements in the social sectors (discussed in Volume III), the NDS suggests improvements to the electricity supply (including the privatisation of the Guyana Electricity Corporation) and to the all-weather road network (especially the Linden-Lethem link). The high cost of transporting raw materials for processing and the undependable power supply are two key constraints to the development of the sector.
- the development of a labour force educated and trained for the modern era.
- the improvement of the policy framework, including the framework for the industrial relations, the tax regime and exchange rate policy.
- the improvement of access to credit through institutions such as the Institute for Private Enterprise Development (IPED).

Science and Technology

- the establishment of a co-ordinating body for science and technology; essentially a new National Science and Research Council with a different definition of its organisation and functions. The NDS also suggests that there needs to be a clear and appropriate ministerial responsibility for science and technology. The co-ordinating body would also be responsible for reviewing the role of information technology in Guyana's development.

Labour and Employment Policy

The NDS aims to reduce unemployment and underemployment and the accompanying poverty by creating greater amounts of productive employment and greater labour flexibility and mobility. The NDS recommends:

- the development of a macroeconomic framework (see Volume II) to accelerate economic growth, which in turn will increase both employment and real wages. The growth path recommended in the NDS is one that is as labour-intensive as possible in the short term. Specific measures would include the promotion of small and micro-enterprises, and the creation of an Export Processing Zone.
- the establishment of a small business development department which will co-ordinate agencies and bodies involved in this sector, work to certify and register businesses, and implement government policies. The NDS also recommends the review of the Companies Act; the creation of legislation to ensure small enterprises pay household and not commercial rates for public utilities; and the waiving of costs associated with the transfer of personal property to a business.
- the development of a highly flexible and trained labour force. This will require a strong focus on technical and vocational education and training (TVET) guided by the needs of the private sector and partially subsidised by a small tax on the industry. The private sector and lending organisations such as IPED should play a central role.
- the increase of Central Government salaries. Two alternatives are setting public sector salaries at 70 to 80% of the private sector salaries in corresponding job classifications and the increasing of real salaries in the

Central Government by 100% over the next 5 years. The NDS also recommends that wages and salaries be linked to performance.

- the establishment of a labour market information system as a basis for formulating, implementing and evaluating human resource policies and training schemes, as well as to give workers timely access to employment information.

- the creation of an industrial relations framework to resolve disputes, including improved structures and procedures for bargaining and a move away from industry-wide bargaining.

Tourism

Guyana possesses vast areas of interior that are still pristine, with untouched forests that are so diverse they can show the entire spectrum of tropical rainforest at its best. The potential for a thriving eco-tourism industry is promising but several key constraints to the sector's development must first be addressed. The NDS recommends:

- a focus on high quality eco-tourism in controlled numbers that do not exceed scientifically determined carrying capacities of interior sites. The NDS also suggests improvements in marketing with better targeting and wider advertising, funded in a joint arrangement between government and the industry.

- the development of the required institutional framework. This will involve laws and behaviour codes for both eco-tourism operators and eco-tourists, as well as for monitoring activities. Since tourism is essentially a private sector enterprise, the NDS recommends the establishment of an incentive regime to attract private sector investment. Also, in all eco-tourism development, priority must be given to Amerindian involvement.

- the establishment of a National Tourist Board. Its main

responsibilities would be regulation, marketing, research, and product development.

- the removal of impediments to investment in the private aircraft industry, and the encouragement of international airlines to come to Guyana.

- investment in infrastructure to support the tourist industry, particularly in relation to airport, airstrip and medical evacuation facilities, visitor security, the prevalence of malaria and the deficiencies in the potable water systems.

THE INFRASTRUCTURE SECTORS (VOLUME 5)

The infrastructure sector is basic to the functioning of any economy, and crucial to the success of Guyana, given its geography and dispersed settlements. A growing economy requires a rapid expansion of capacity and improvements in efficiency in the areas of electricity generation and transmission; all modes of transportation; water supply and drainage; and sea defences. Guyana faces a number of bottlenecks in the infrastructure sectors, damaging the economy's ability to grow and the country's ability to compete on the world market.

Transport Development

The transport sector is critical to Guyana's economic development. The NDS looks at the areas of road, maritime, and air transport and makes various recommendations:

Road Transport

The road system in Guyana - which has played a central role in the country's development - faces a number of constraints, which the NDS seeks to address. The NDS suggests:

- investment to rehabilitate and expand the paved road system.

- the development of all-weather road links to mining, forest, and agriculture areas to facilitate development.
- the completion of the Lethem-Georgetown road link. This will facilitate the economic development of the southern parts of the country, and create opportunities for trade with neighbouring regions in Brazil.
- investment in the construction of bridges across major rivers. Specifically, the NDS calls for the construction of a bridge across the Berbice River.
- the encouragement of private sector involvement in the sector
- the institutional strengthening of the Road Administration Division (RAD).
- the introduction of measures to improve safety levels.

Maritime Transport

With the decentralisation of economic activity and the corresponding development of the interior regions of the country, there is an increasing demand for water transport in Guyana. The NDS makes recommendations to overcome the various constraints faced by the sector:

- the development of a deep water harbour. This is seen as critical to support to the recommended Export Processing Zone, as well as the rapidly expanding exports of bulk goods, such as rice, sugar and new kinds of wood products.
- the strengthening of the ports and harbours system. The NDS calls for improvements to the administration of the ports and harbours; measures to increase the efficiency of the port handling systems; and investment to enhance aids to navigation in harbours.
- the reform of the Transport and Harbours Department and its incorporation in the National Port Authority.
- the strengthening of safety standards regarding coastal, regional and international shipping

Air Transport

As with the other two areas of transportation, air transportation is vital to the economic development of the country. In addition, air transport plays a vital role in linking the coastal areas and hinterland communities, many of which are inaccessible by any other means of transportation. The NDS recommends:

- a review of civil aviation legislation in light of the evolving changes in the aviation environment locally and internationally. The NDS also suggest the ratification of major international conventions on civil aviation.
- the upgrade and expansion of airport facilities and navigational aids, many of which are in a deteriorated state.
- the encouragement of private sector involvement in the sector.
- the introduction of measures to encourage international airlines to fly to Guyana, including the expansion of the international airport.
- the establishment of an Airport Authority for the co-ordination and management of the international airport and other facilities.
- the establishment of an effective and fully equipped Search and Rescue Unit within the air transport sector to provide emergency services

Energy Policies

If Guyana is to realise its very considerable development potential, a reliable system of electricity generation and transmission is essential. An inadequate system raises the costs of production in all sectors of the economy - particularly for small producers - by requiring companies to install their own generating capacity and by damaging equipment through severe voltage fluctuations. This acts as a discouragement to potential investors. In addition, a poor electricity supply effects a wide cross-section of households. The NDS makes recommendations to overcome the various constraints faced in the sector, and to create a system capable of dealing with the growing energy demands of an expanding economy:

- the upgrade of the transmission and distribution system.
- the encouragement of private sector participation in the power sector, including the participatory privatisation of the Guyana Electricity Corporation (GEC).
- the consideration of alternative energy sources, such as mini-hydro, wind and solar.
- the establishment of a Guyana Energy Agency for national energy planning, including the development of an energy conservation programme.
- the strengthening of the Public Utilities Commission's capacity to regulate the sector.

Water Management and Flood Control

Guyana's geography make effective water management and flood control crucial. The coastal area of Guyana - where most of the population lives and where the main crops are cultivated - lies below sea level and is subjected to flooding and erosion. The NDS makes several recommendations to deal with the problems facing the country's sea defences and drainage and irrigation (D&I) system. The NDS also considers the important role of the hydrometeorological service, which evaluates the country's climate and water resources, and operates the National Meteorological Station Network (NMSN) and the National Hydrological Station Network (NHSN).

Sea Defences

- the rehabilitation of critical coastal protection structures, and the maintenance of the existing infrastructure.
- the reorganisation and strengthening of the Sea and River

Defence Board. The NDS also suggests the establishment of a Shorezone Management Unit.

- the reduction of construction costs for sea defences. The NDS suggests examining means of reducing the costs of production and supply of rocks to sites, including a review of current designs.
- the protection of mangroves. The past failure to protect mangroves has contributed to the deterioration of the sea defences. The NDS calls for a gradual mangrove reforestation programme.

Drainage & Irrigation

- the rehabilitation and maintenance of D&I works. Inadequate maintenance of drainage works reduces yields and keeps some agricultural land out of production.
- a review of legislation governing the management and operation of D&I.
- the institutional strengthening of the sector. The NDS calls for an institutional framework which identifies clear policy objectives; ensures adequate supervision and co-ordination; prevents overlapping jurisdictions between agencies; and specifies clear roles for each agency. The NDS recommends that the national D&I Board take a lead in developing the new institutional structure.
- the encouragement of farmer participation in the development, operation and maintenance of an efficient D&I system, through local Water Users' Associations. The current lack of participation of users in decisions on maintenance has undermined the effectiveness of the drainage and irrigation systems. The NDS also calls for the strengthening of the Local Government Authorities to administer local D&I systems where farmers are satisfied with the current institutional arrangement.

Hydrometeorological Service

- the upgrade of existing stations; improved communication links to data collection centres; automation of stations; and staff training.
- the introduction of measures to strengthen the financial position of the hydrometeorogical service, including the introduction of charges to users (such as airports and the media).

END NOTE
1. www.guyana.org/NDS/nds_summary.htm

A SELECT BIBLIOGRAPHY.

Amoo, S. G. (1997), *The Challenge of Ethnicity and Conflicts in Africa: The Need for a New Paradigm,* New York, UNDP.

Apter, D. E. (ed.), (1997), *The Legitimization of Violence,* London, Macmillan.

Arendt, Hannah, (1958), *The Human Condition,* Cambridge, Cambridge University Press.

Barber, B. R. (1984), *Strong Democracy: Participatory Politics for a New Age,* London, University of California Press.

Bastian, S. and Luckham, R. (eds.) (2003), *Can Democracy be Designed?,* London, Zed Books Ltd.

Botwinick, A.and Connolly,W.E. (eds.) *Democracy and Vision / Sheldon Wolin and the vicissitudes of the political,* Princeton, Princeton University Press.

Burton, J. (1982), *Dear Survivors,* London, Pinter.

Burton, J. (1997), *Violence Explained*, Manchester, Manchester University Press.

Chan, Sylvia, (2002), *Liberalism, Democracy and Development,* Cambridge, Cambridge

Chase, A. (1994), *Guyana; A Nation in Transit, Burnham's Role,* Georgetown, Pavnikpress.

Chryssochoou, D. N. (2001), *Theorizing European Integration,* London, Sage Publications University Press.

Claude, I. L. (1964), *Swords into Ploughshares,* New York, Random House.

Dahl, R. A. (1990), *After The Revolution? Authority in a Good Society,* London, Yale University Press.

Dahl, R. A. (1999), *On Democracy,* London, Yale University Press.

Ferguson, T. (1995), *Structural Adjustment and Good Governance: The Case of Guyana*, Georgetown, Guyana National Printers.

Ferguson, T. (1999), *To Survive Sensibly or to Court Heroic Death: Management of Guyana's Political Economy 1965-85,* Georgetown, Guyana National Printers.

Francis, Diana. (2002), *People, Peace and Power,* London, Pluto Press.

Fukuyama, F. (1992), *The End of History and The Last Man,* London, Penguin.

Fukuyama, F. (1995), *Trust: The Social Virtues and the Creation of Prosperity,* NY, NY, Simon and Shuster Inc.

Fukuyama, F. (2004), *State Building*, London, Profile Books Ltd

Gagnon, Alain-G. and Tully, J. (eds.), (2001), *Multinational Democracies,* Cambridge, Cambridge University Press.

Gray, J. (2000), *Two Faces of Liberalism*, Cambridge, Polity Press.

Gray, J. (2002), *Straw Dogs*, London, Granta Books

Gray, J. (2003), *Al Qaeda And What It Means To Be Modern*, London, Faber and Faber Ltd.

Glaser, D.(2001), *Politics and Society in South Africa,* London, Sage Publications.

Gutmann, Amy (2003), *Identity in Democracy,* Oxford, Princeton University Press.

Hodges, M. (ed.) (1972), *European Integration,* Harmondsworth, Penguin.

Ignatieff, M. (2003) *Empire Lite*, London, Vintage.

Jagan, C. (1975), *The West on Trial: The Fight for Guyana's Freedom.* Berlin, Seven Seas Publishers.

Karran, K. (ed) (2004), *Racial Conflict and Power Sharing in Guyana.* Belle Vue, Offerings Publications.

Keane, J. (1998), *Civil Society,* Cambridge, Polity Press.

Knight, B., Chigudu, H. and Tandon, M. (2002), *Reviving Democracy: Citizens at the Heart of Governance,* London Earthscan.

Kymlicka, W. (1977), *Multicultural Citizenship: A Liberal Theory Of Minority Rights,* Oxford, Clarendon Press.

Kymlicka, W. (1990), *Contemporary Political Philosophy,* Oxford, Oxford University Press.

Lederach, J. P. (1997), *Building Peace,* Washington, D.C., U.S. Institute of Peace Press.

Lewis, W. A. (1965), *Politics in West Africa,* London, Allen & Unwin.

Lijphart, A. (1977), *Democracy in Plural Societies,* London, Yale University Press.

Lijphart, A. (1999), *Patterns of Democracy,* London, Yale University Press.

Margalit, A. (1996), *The Decent Society,* London, Harvard University Press.

Mill, J, S. (1861), *Considerations on Representative Government*, London, J. M. Dent & Son, (1910).

Mitrany, D. (1943*), A Working Peace System*, Chicago, Quadrangle.

Montville, J. V, (ed.) (1991), *Conflict and Peacemaking in Multiethnic Societies,* New York, Macmillan.

Nascimento, C. A. and Burrowes, R. A. (eds.), *A Destiny to Mould: Selected Discourses by The Prime Minister Of Guyana,* London, Longman.

Nicholls, D. (1974), *Three Varieties of Pluralism,* London, Macmillan.

Pateman, Carole, (1970), *Participation and Democratic Theory,* Cambridge, Cambridge University Press.

Popper, K. R. (1957), *The Poverty of Historicism,* London, Routledge and Kegan Paul.

Popper, K. R. (1965), *The Open Society and its Enemies,* London, Routledge and Kegan Paul.

Popper, K. R. (1993), *In Search of a Better World,* London, Routledge.

Popper, K. R. (1999), *All Life is Problem Solving,* London Routledge

Premdas, R, (2001), 'Ethno-Racial Divisions and Governance', *Racism and Public Policy,* (Conference Paper), Geneva, UNRISD.

Premdas, R.R. (1995), *Ethnic Conflict and Development: The Case of Guyana,* Aldershot, Avebury.

Rambushka, A. ans Shepsle, H. (eds.) (1972),*Politics in Plural Societies: A Theory of Democratic Instability,* Columbus, Merrill.

Reilly, B. (2001), *Democracy in Divided Societies,* Cambridge, Cambridge University Press.

Sandel, M. (1996), *Democracy's Discontent,* Camb., Mass., Belknap Press

Schumpeter, J. A. (1943), *Capitalism, Socialism and Democracy,* London, Allen & Unwin.

Seecoomar, J. (2002), *Contributions Towards the Resolution of Conflict in Guyana,* Leeds, Peepal Tree Press.

Sen, A. (1999), *Development as Freedom,* Oxford, Oxford University Press.

Sewell, J. P. (1966), *Functionalism and World Politics,* Princeton, N. J., Princeton University Press.

Shahabuddeen, M. (1978), *Constitutional Development in Guyana 1621 – 1978,* Georgetown.

Sites, P. (1973), *Control: The Basis Of Social Order,* New York, Dunellen.

Taylor, C. (1992), 'The Politics of Recognition', in Gutmann, A. (ed.), *Multiculturalism and the Politics of Recognition,* Princeton, Princeton University Press.

Taylor, C. (1996) *The Passion Of The Western Mind,* London, Pimlico.

Uhr, J. (2003), *Creating a Culture Of Integrity,* London, Commonwealth Secretariat.

Young, Iris, M. (1990), *Justice and the Politics of Difference,* Princeton, Princeton University Press.

Young, Iris, M. (2000), *Inclusion and Democracy,* Oxford, Oxford University Press.

INDEX

ALSO BY JUDAMAN SEECOOMAR

Judaman Seecoomar
Contributions Towards the Resolution of Conflict in Guyana
ISBN: 9781900715652; pp. 304; pub. 2002; £14.99

From 1955 onwards, when the anti-colonial movement split into competing ethnic sections, conflict between African and Indian Guyanese has held Guyana in a deadlock which has undermined all attempts at social and economic development. At its height exploding into civil war in the 1960s, the constant state of tension has led to rigged elections, authoritarian government, economic collapse and driven hundreds of thousands of Guyanese to emigrate. Even in the present, when for the first time for decades, free and fair elections can be held, winning and losing further divides the nation.

Judaman Seecoomar's book offers an analysis of how Guyana has arrived at this impasse and suggests a process that could lead out of it. He identifies a history of authoritarian government where those who control the state (whether colonial governments in the past, those who seized power through rigged elections, or those who gained it by virtue of having the support of the ethnic majority), have responded to Guyana's cultural pluralism by suppressing or ignoring the interests of the minority. He argues that the failure to satisfy the human needs of all Guyana's ethnic groups is the root cause of conflict and only their satisfaction offers a means of harnessing all the nation's energies for development. He identifies the crucial needs as being those that relate to security, the recognition of cultural identity, participation in decision-making and the fair distribution of social rewards.

The book looks to the developing practice of conflict resolution through strategies of collaborative problem solving. It argues that such a process would offer Guyana the means of finding constitutional and institutional arrangements acceptable to all ethnic groups. It provides both an account of the theoretical frameworks for such an approach and case studies of conflict resolution in action, such as in Northern Ireland. It documents the initial attempts by the Caribbean Community (CARICOM) to broker talks between the main Guyanese political parties.

In a world where internal conflict in multi-ethnic states is the major source of regional instability, this is a timely book.